MINA'S STORY :
A DOCTOR'S MEMOIR
OF THE HOLOCAUST

MINA'S STORY
A Doctor's Memoir of the Holocaust

DR. MINA DEUTSCH

Toronto: ECW PRESS 1994

Copyright © Dr. Mina Deutsch, 1994

All rights reserved.

CANADIAN CATALOGUING IN PUBLICATION DATA

Deutsch, Mina, 1911–
  Mina's story : a doctor's memoir of the holocaust

ISBN 1-55022-212-0

1. Deutsch, Mina, 1911– . 2. Holocaust, Jewish (1939–1945) –
Poland – Personal narratives. 3. Physicians, Jewish – Poland –
Biography. I. Title.

DS135.P63D48 1994   940.53'18'092   C94-930853-6

COVER ILLUSTRATION: High school graduation picture given to
the author's late husband several months after they met as medical
students at the university in Prague, with the following inscription:
*To the boy — of my youth / To the boy —whom I like / Prague, February
15, 1932.*

This book has been published with the assistance of
The Canada Council, and the Ontario Arts Council.

Design and imaging by ECW Type & Art, Oakville, Ontario.
Printed by Kromar Printing, Winnipeg, Manitoba.

Distributed in Canada by General Distribution Services,
30 Lesmill Road, Toronto, Ontario M3B 2T6.

Distributed in the United States by General Distribution Services,
4600 Witmer Industrial Estates, #4, Niagara Falls, New York, 14305.

International distribution by Bailey Distribution, Learoyd Road,
Mountfield Road Ind Est, New Romney, Kent, England TW28 8XO.

Published by ECW PRESS,
2120 Queen Street East, Suite 200, Toronto, Ontario M4E 1E2.

*To the memory of my late husband,
Dr. Leon Deutsch,
who shared these experiences with me,
and to that of our families who
perished during the Holocaust.*

FOREWORD

For many years after the war, in our conversations, thoughts, and dreams, we always returned to the subject of what we went through, all the relatives we lost, and how these horrible experiences affected us. When my daughter grew older and especially after the grandchildren were born, she insisted that I write about all the memories we often talked about, so that the grandchildren would know what hardships it is possible to overcome, and what seemingly impossible tragedies could be perpetrated by members of a nation that was considered to be highly cultured and that had previously been widely admired and emulated.

I was also encouraged to write this book by my good friend and colleague, Professor Karolina Jus, who was at the time a Professor of Psychiatry at McGill University. She herself had tried to record her memoirs, but was unable to do so since she found her recollections of the past too painful and depressing. She insisted that I was of a stronger character and would be able to do what she could not bring herself to attempt.

As my grandchildren grew to an age when they became interested in their roots and recent history, I decided to complete these remembrances. I hope they will remain as a memorial to my family who perished at the hands of the Nazi murderers, a tribute to the simple people who helped us at the peril of their own lives, and as a record of our times for future generations.

ACKNOWLEDGEMENTS

I would like to thank Jennifer Kane-Weiner for her invaluable assistance in editing the manuscript. I also wish to thank my daughter and son-in-law, Eva and Fred, and my grandchildren Lisa, Anne, and Mark for their help and support.

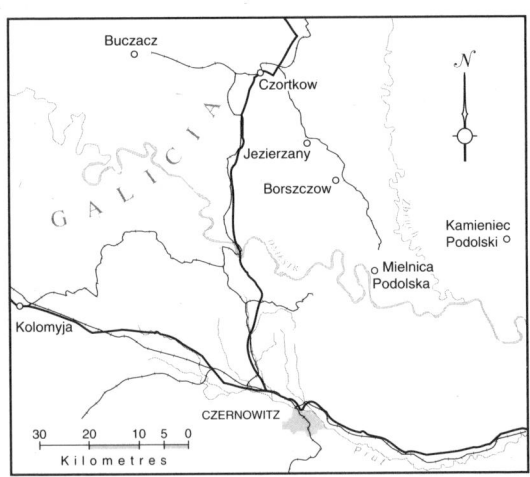

Detail of area shaded in map above.

1

I WAS BORN Mina Kimmel on 24 December 1911, in Jezierżany, a small town in Eastern Poland that belonged to Austria at the time. I was the fifth in a family of six children, two boys and four girls. We were all very close. When one of us got a bar of chocolate, we would never eat it ourselves but would divide it into six equal pieces, one for each child.

My oldest sister, Lottie, was a beautiful girl who loved to read. She married Mendel Schaffer, a handsome, intelligent, reliable man. Mendel was a good businessman and managed the export of wheat and eggs to Germany and Italy. He also owned a lot of fields and woods. Mendel and Lottie had two children: Markus, who was as handsome as his father, and Eva, a likeable girl. In 1940, Mendel was taken to Siberia by the Russians because he was considered a bourgeois. He perished there. Lottie, 18-year-old Markus, and 13-year-old Eva were killed during an action by the Germans in the Borszczów ghetto in 1943.

Next came my brother Willy, who was fortunate to have left Poland for Canada in 1930, thereby escaping the war. He married Lily Pedovitch in Montreal and they had two children, Earl and Miriam.

My sister Rachel married Baruch Goldig, a Hebrew scholar. He was a sociable man who could keep people involved in conversation for hours. Rachel had had many suitors, but she had refused them all. That is, until she was introduced to Baruch by a matchmaker and they soon married. They had a son, Philip, who was nine years old when we brought them into our hiding place during the war.

My sister Regina and I were very close. We were in the same grade at school for some time. She married a fine, handsome man and they had one son, Julek. They perished when their hiding place, an abandoned house, was discovered by the Germans. Rachel and Baruch had been hiding in the same place but were not discovered.

The youngest of the family was Levi, a helpful and considerate boy who always tried to make life easier for people who needed help. He worked in my father's business and was relied on a great deal. He was very bright and imaginative and had good ideas. From the time I taught him to walk, we had always been very close.

My parents were Pesach and Taube (Liebling) Kimmel. My father was very devoted to our family but quite strict with the children. Once, in the three years of Russian rule during World War I, soldiers forced my brother Willy to help build a road not far from our house. He and other boys his age had to crush stones to cover the ground. Most of the parents were afraid to stand up to the Russian authorities, and allowed their children to be taken away to work without a struggle. My father followed my brother to the work site and brought him home. My mother always told us what a remarkable man he was. She herself had other good qualities: she was quiet, composed, good-hearted, and always ready to help the needy. She was a confidante to us children and often helped us to get father's approval.

Poor people often came to our house asking for food, a few pennies, or some clothes, and I cannot recall a time when my mother let anyone leave empty-handed. She would also visit the people in town who had lost their jobs but were too ashamed to beg, and she made sure that they accepted some food or money to get by until her next visit.

I can remember some of the last year of World War I. We suffered from lack of food and clothing, and were frequently startled by Russian soldiers bursting into our home at all hours of the day and night. They beat up my father, and on one occasion, even my grandmother, because when they asked for forks to eat the Sabbath dinner she had made for us, she told them: "Lords like you can eat with your fingers." The Russians made themselves at home with us; they slept in our beds, ate whatever food they could find, and took whatever they wanted with them when they left.

Around that time my mother developed a bleeding gastric ulcer and was unable to take care of us. She was weak and emaciated and had to spend most of her time in bed since we had no special diet or medical help for her. My maternal grandmother, who was in her eighties, managed to look after her and the rest of the household.

The last night of the Russian retreat remains vivid in my memory. Russian soldiers rushed from house to house in the Jewish section of town, setting fire to homes and killing everyone they came across. A friend of my parents was hiding in her garden when she saw them setting fire to her house. When they left, she managed to put out the fire with a few pails of water. A short time later, the Russians returned, found her there, and pierced her heart with a bayonet. The sound of her seven small children crying at her funeral the next day was almost unbearable.

My own family managed to escape to a nearby garbage dump, a hill covered with weeds and bushes, where we lay noiselessly all night in the mud and stench. We watched the Russian soldiers gallop by on their horses, hollering wildly, as they searched for people to kill. The next morning came silence. My father went out to investigate and returned with the good news that the Russians were gone and our house had been spared. Since we lived in the outskirts of town, and the Russians had apparently retreated in a hurry, they had not even reached our street. We ourselves did not fare as well: despite our efforts to clean off the mud and garbage that clung to our bodies, we developed large purulent sores that took a long time to heal.

After the war, Poland once again became a state. My father tried to reopen his grain business to support our large family. It had been a sizeable, prosperous enterprise that he had founded before I was born, and he was now beginning again to export grain to Italy and Germany. He was an energetic businessman, but times were difficult and everything was scarce. He had many business dealings in another town, Mielnica Podolska, which was about three hours away by train. No matter how much he was away from home during the week, however, he always returned for the Sabbath.

Our lives gradually returned to normal. However, during the summer when I was nine, there was a big fire in Jezierżany, started accidentally by a farmer who was harvesting his crops. Twenty-four homes were destroyed, including ours. Since my father had become more and more involved with his business in Mielnica, he decided to move our family there. He bought us a nice home, where we were comfortable and happy for the next few years. At first I was lonely for my friends and school, but this did not last long.

I continued in grades four through seven at a public school in Mielnica, where I did well. I also attended an excellent Hebrew school where I learned to speak fluent Hebrew. During the Christmas holidays of the year I was in seventh grade, my father's brother Benny came to visit us from New York. He was especially eager to see my paternal grandmother, who was about 90 years old at the time. We enjoyed Benny's visit. He was a charming, wise, and pleasant man. He was also a millionaire from his Fifth Avenue fur business, and showered us with gifts. He did a lot for the poor people in town, supported the Jewish cemetery, and donated money for the renovation of the synagogue his parents attended. As promised, he later sent us his family for the summer, and we had a wonderful time travelling around the countryside with my aunt Paulina and cousins Charlie and Sarah.

After I graduated from elementary school at the age of 13, my parents decided to send me to high school in Lwów. I was to stay with my aunt Cecilia and uncle Jacob who lived there. I started in a private high school called Karpowny, but my aunt died suddenly of a heart attack toward the end of my first year, so my father sent me to live with his close friend and business associate, Moses Pohoryles. That home became my second home. I loved the Pohoryles family like my own, and I think they felt the same about me. Moreover, my father was in Lwów once a week on business, which helped ease my feelings of homesickness during those first years away. Adela, Moses' wife, reminded me of my mother. She was always relaxed and smiling and took a great interest in what the children were doing.

Moses and Adela had two daughters, Anda and Tońcia, and a son named Samuel. Anda was two or three years younger than I was and I always helped her with her homework so that she was well-prepared for school. Each summer vacation she came home with me to visit my parents. Tońcia was a quiet girl who liked to go to movies, the theatre, and the opera. About a year before the war broke out, she married a very nice man. Samuel, who was much older than his sisters, was always busy with his father's business.

After I joined the Pohoryleses, I attended a very exclusive private high school called "Zofja Strzalkowska." When I graduated, I decided to study medicine. I dreamed of helping people who were suffering and in need of attention. I especially wanted to help children, and believed that women were better suited to be paediatricians than men since we have a more gentle way with youngsters. I applied to the Medical Faculty of Lwów, although only a fraction of a percent of Jewish men were accepted and, as a Jewess, I knew it was useless. I then applied to the Karlova University in Prague, Czechoslovakia, where I was accepted. After one year there, I transferred to the German University in Prague, which had a better reputation and where I was more at ease since my German was fluent.

Life was marvellous in the golden city of Prague in the early 1930s. People were free. The streets were almost as busy during the night as they were during the day. I loved the university, my social life, outings to all parts of the city, the theatres, operas, concerts, restaurants, student clubs, and walks on the "Vaclawskie Namesti," the main street in Prague. After just a few days there, I met my future husband, Leon Deutsch, at the student centre, the "Studentsky Domov." We met playing ping-pong. He was a good-looking man, tall, slim, with black hair and dark-brown eyes. He was from Przemyśl and was one year ahead of me in medical school. Leon loved to travel and to sightsee, and we visited many places together: Pirkenhammer, with its famous porcelain, crystal, and glass factories; the resorts of Marienbad and Francensbad; and many other interesting places. After we had known each other for about two years, we went to visit his mother in Karlsbad, a resort where she spent every summer. In 1937, when Leon graduated from medical school, we became engaged. On the way home for summer vacation that year, we visited the rest of his family in Przemyśl.

Leon's father Moses was a very prominent businessman who owned a chemical fertilizer factory, one of two of its kind in Poland. He was very intelligent, and was well-respected in the community. Frania Grünfeld, Leon's mother, was an elegant woman who kept a meticulous house with the help of a number of servants. Leon's maternal grandmother, Chaya Frank, was very devoted to him and helped to bring up the children. Romek, his older brother, helped his father with the business. His younger sister, Ida, was a most beautiful girl.

After the vacation, we both returned to Prague: I to finish my last year of medical school and Leon to begin a year of internal medicine. Conditions at the university had changed dramatically by then. German students greeted professors with cries of "Heil Hitler," and the professors responded in kind. In class, front-row seats were occupied only by German students, who ignored even those Jews whom they had previously befriended. We were told that only those Jewish students in their last year of studies would be permitted to complete their final examinations; all others could not continue at all. Moreover, only Jewish professors were to administer exams to the Jewish students.

It was then that we realized that there was nothing further for us in Prague. The threat of Hitler was an imminent one, so we decided to return to Poland. Leon and I were married at the home of the Chazins, distant relatives and good friends, in Lwów in September, 1938. Julius Chazin was a lawyer, and the only Jew in the Polish opera. His wife was a very clever woman and the force behind many of his successes. Our wedding and the exquisite dinner that followed took place in the Chazins' elegant home. After a short honeymoon in a nearby resort, we went to Mielnica to visit my family over the High Holidays. Then we came to Przemyśl, and made a temporary home in one of the buildings belonging to my in-laws' factory.

We lived across the street from a general hospital where we intended to obtain further training in internal medicine, though no salary was promised.

We spent the fall and winter of 1938 working there, and in the spring of 1939 we were accepted by a psychiatric hospital called Zofjówka in Otwock, a suburb of Warsaw. Zofjówka had very qualified physicians on staff, including Dr. Frostik, who was the founder of insulin shock treatment, and Dr. Gustav Bychowski, who later became a well-known psychoanalyst in New York. As the clinical director of the hospital, his lectures were the most interesting. We learned a great deal about psychiatry there and planned to stay for a while. Moreover, we were expecting our first child by then, and had found an obstetrician and hospital in Warsaw. However, things did not turn out as expected.

2

WORLD WAR II broke out and the mobilization of troops began. Since Leon expected to be drafted at any time and did not want to leave me alone during my last month of pregnancy, we decided to return to Przemyśl to stay with his family. Our trip there was a frightening one.

When we reached the extremely crowded train station in Warsaw, we had to push through masses of people just to obtain information about our departure. We were very careful to stay together, since it would have been nearly impossible to find one another if we had been separated. Every train that arrived or departed was full of soldiers, who had priority, and only a very few civilians managed to squeeze on. After standing in the dark for many hours, we managed to board a train headed in our direction. We travelled, still in darkness, sitting on top of our suitcases. Early the next morning, we realized the train had stopped moving. We got off and were terrified to see that we were the only ones left in the coach: the main part of the train and the rest of the coaches full of soldiers had gone on without us. We were abandoned in the middle of a field with no one in sight. We stayed near the coach, hoping that another train would pass by and pick us up, but it didn't.

We spent the day waiting in the scorching sun, without food or water, until we realized that we had to do something before night set in. We set out through the field — in an unknown direction — until we reached a road. We continued walking until we came across a man who told us that the train station was quite a distance away. We begged him to help us reach it, and offered him money to do so. The man said that his horses had been confiscated and that all he could do for us was to bring us a small hand wagon to carry our luggage while we walked. He also promised to bring us some bread and water. We prayed that he meant what he said; in such times, you could not trust anyone. We even had the fleeting thought that he might come back with someone else and try to rob or kill us. Such occurrences were not uncommon in Poland. However, we had no choice other than to believe him.

Thus, we were very relieved when the man returned after a while with the wagon and food. We started out for the station. It was almost dark when we arrived, and none of the many people waiting there knew if a train would be coming or not. Luckily, a freight train passed through during the night and we managed to get on board.

We reached Przemyśl by morning. The city was under siege, and every few minutes we had to run from the third floor of my inlaws' building to take shelter in the basement — not an easy task for me in my ninth month of pregnancy. After a few days, it became clear that the Germans were going to take over. Panic was great; everyone tried to move east as quickly as possible, but there were no means of transportation of any kind since all vehicles had been confiscated by the military. Although we knew it was dangerous to travel by train, which were constantly bombed, we decided (along with my brother-in-law Romek) to do so anyway. The trains travelled only at night to avoid being spotted by German planes. Late that night we boarded one headed east. We hoped to reach my parents in Mielnica on the Russian-Rumanian border of Poland, which we knew would take about 20 hours by train. However, early the next morning, as we reached Sambor, which was only about three hours from Przemyśl, our train was bombed.

The car we were travelling in was so extremely crowded that we had had to stand the whole way with our legs partly hanging out of the open door. Machine-gun fire fell around us like hail, and it was only a miracle that we were not hurt. When we finally managed to get out of our coach, we were faced with a bloody, horrible sight: the train's engine was destroyed, and in the next car 26 people were killed and many others wounded. German planes circled overhead, and we feared that the bombing would begin again. We ran toward the city, leaving our belongings behind. It was a great distance from the station to the city and when we reached the outskirts of town, I fainted.

Once we were in Sambor, my brother-in-law helped us find a place to stay. He knew of a lawyer who told us that the owners of the nicest villa in town had escaped to the east, and he managed to get us a key to their home. The next day, however, the Germans took over the villa and forced us into one room, forbidding us to leave. My brother-in-law happened to be outside at the time, and the guards refused to let him back in. After two days, we noticed that a German general and several officers had occupied the upper floor of the villa. The rooms on the lower floor were converted into business offices, and typewriters could be heard working uninterruptedly all day.

Late one afternoon a Russian general and a group of officers arrived at the villa. The officers ran back and forth from the general's quarters to the business offices. In the morning, the Germans were gone and the Russians had taken over the villa. An agreement had apparently been reached between the Russian and the German generals whereby the Russians would take over Przemyśl to the River San. This became the new border, and the part of Przemyśl called Zasanie now belonged to the Germans.

We told the Russian officers what had happened to us and asked them to let us go. After some deliberations, they released us. My brother-in-law knew of an elderly lady, a distant relative, who lived in a modest house nearby, and said she would be pleased to have us stay with her. We were with her for a few weeks, but were eager to return to Przemyśl since I was expecting to give birth very soon. We had a difficult time returning to Przemyśl. It was impossible to find transportation, and we kept hearing that the roads were not safe for travel since ammunition had been left scattered on them, and along the fields. People were killed from accidentally stumbling upon them.

We had left all our belongings at the station in Sambor and had never recovered them. It was therefore difficult to acquire any underwear or change of clothing. It was also extremely difficult to get any food, and we were hungry most of the time. We worried about both of our families, from whom we had received no news. When the first trains began to travel between Sambor and Przemyśl, we left. Just before our departure, we heard rumours that the Germans had murdered a few hundred prominent Jews before leaving Przemyśl. We had no way of knowing if my father-in-law was among them. A few days later we ran into my husband's uncle, Isaac, from Strzyżów, who confirmed the rumours. He said he also was worried about his brother, but it had been impossible for him to get into the centre of the city to see him. He had had to hide in the outlying fields instead. (Isaac was eventually taken into the Russian army and sent as deep into Russia as Kazakhstan. After the war, he lived with us for a few months in Katowice. His wife and three children perished during the Holocaust.)

3

WHEN WE ARRIVED in Przemyśl, we immediately saw the sadness on the faces of Fanny and Ida, my mother- and sister-in-law, and we knew that they were trying to hide something. They tried to tell us that my father-in-law was away on business, but Leon soon discovered what had really happened to him. The Gestapo had asked the Jewish Council (Judenradt) for a list of 250 prominent male doctors, lawyers, executives, and others. My father-in-law's name, Moses Mendel, was on the list. When they came to get him, he happened not to be at home. The Gestapo told Fanny where to send him when he returned, and threatened to harm her if he did not show up. When Moses came home and heard what had happened, he immediately decided to obey their orders for fear that they would return and carry out their threat to Fanny. He was never seen again. Before the Germans retreated behind the River San, they took all 250 men out to a nearby forest and shot them. Then they poured lime over their bodies so that they were unrecognizable. Fanny and Ida had to go identify Moses since Leon, Romek, and I were in Sambor at the time. They had a terrible time doing so, and after searching through corpses for an entire day were able to recognize him only by a sock on his foot. The rest of his body and his clothes had been destroyed by the lime.

Fanny and Ida suffered horrible guilt over Moses's gruesome death. They blamed themselves for letting him report to the Gestapo, and believed that they should have gone off to hide with him instead, since the next day the Germans retreated and the Soviets took over Przemyśl.

Under those sad circumstances, in a house filled with mourning, a scarcity of food, and no means of heating, our daughter Eva came into the world. It was exactly one month after Moses had been murdered. She was born at home, since all the hospitals had been taken over by the military. We had no way to even warm up a little water, and she could not be given her first bath until many hours later when Leon cut up some crates to make a fire.

In comparison to many other people, however, we were fortunate: we had a roof over our heads. Thousands of refugees lay in the streets around our house during the cold October nights, feeding their infants crumbs of black bread soaked in water. They often approached us for water, the only thing we could give them. Weeks passed while they waited for permission from the Germans to return to their homes behind the River San, as far away as Warsaw.

Meanwhile, the Soviets had started their activities. There were denunciations from some of the workers in my father-in-law's factory, which was located in Zasanie behind the River San. Although this was in the hands of the Germans, the Russian police (N.K.V.D.) came to our house, which was in Przemyśl proper. They molested Fanny, searched the house, and stole everything of value. They claimed that my father-in-law was a bourgeois and that we had lived long enough on the sweat of the workers; the time had come for the workers to take over the house and live more comfortably.

We foresaw the difficulties that awaited us, particularly Fanny, so we decided to move to Lwów. I had grown up there and still had relatives and many friends living there. It was also not too far from Przemyśl. Fortunately, we knew that the Soviets would not try to follow us; no matter how guilty they considered you of "bourgeois" crimes, they never tried to chase you once you escaped. Leon went to Lwów first to find a place for us to live. This was a difficult task, since Lwów had grown from 300,000 inhabitants before the war to more than 1,000,000 after the Soviets took over. In addition to rent, one had to pay several thousand złotys in so-called "key money" to the person living in a place to evacuate it. After several weeks, Leon found us a place, but was afraid to leave it to come pick us up because someone might break in and take it over while he was gone.

My in-laws helped me pack our belongings, and my brother-in-law Romek planned to take me and six-week-old Eva by bus to Lwów. Ida got up at four in the morning to save some seats for us, though the bus was due to depart only at nine. There was already a crowd of people trying to board, and Ida, who was very delicate, was afraid she would be squeezed to death. Finally, she managed to reserve a seat for me and the baby. My brother-in-law had to stand for the entire ten-hour trip.

I will remember that trip for the rest of my life. It was a cold and windy December day. The windows in the bus were broken and the air was very drafty. Eva was wet and hungry and cried most of the trip. I tried to get her a bottle from my bag but couldn't reach it because people were lying all over my things. The wetness came through her blanket.

When we arrived, Leon and my best friend, Tońcia Pohoryles, were waiting at the terminal. They tried to find a way to bring us and our luggage to the apartment, over an hour away, but it was very difficult. Finally, when all the passengers had left, my brother-in-law approached the bus driver and asked him to take us home. He agreed to do it for a price. When we arrived at the apartment at about nine o'clock that evening, I went straight inside and changed Eva's diaper. She immediately quieted down and I could almost feel her relief.

Life was difficult, but not compared to the hardships we experienced after the outbreak of the war. The Russians brought with them in 1939 a Siberian winter and a great scarcity of fuel. Our apartment consisted of three rooms and a large kitchen. Shortly after we moved in, the largest room was confiscated by a Russian officer and his wife and child, who also used our kitchen. We and Eva shared a little room that we heated slightly. The rest of the apartment, including the second room, which was occupied by my brother and brother-in-law, remained cold all winter.

We always had to stand in line for whatever food was available in the stores. There were two lines: one for mothers with babies, and a much longer one for everyone else. If I knew there was something I wanted in a store, I took Eva in her carriage and went to stand in line, no matter how bad the weather. For babies and children, there were sometimes special items. (In general, children are favoured in the Soviet Union. When one travels by train, for example, there is a special, more comfortable coach for those with children. I experienced this luxury when I went from Lwów to Jezierżany to visit my parents, about 18 hours by train. The train was so overcrowded that people were sitting on the steps and roofs of the coaches, but because I had a child with me, I was led into a nicely decorated private coach.)

Despite the fact that three men in the house had jobs, it was difficult to make ends meet. Because there were not many items to be had in the government stores, we were compelled from time to time to buy on the black market. This was very expensive; every so often we had to sell some of our precious belongings there.

We became accustomed to our way of life. I don't think we complained; we needed very little. Then suddenly, on a beautiful sunny morning in the spring of 1941, shooting was heard. People rushed out into the streets, confused and wondering what would happen next. Some thought it was a military manoeuvre; others were sure that the Germans had taken over Przemyśl and were approaching Lwów. After a few hours, the latter proved correct: the Soviets were hastily retreating. Many people wanted to escape with them, but were refused due to lack of transportation. Towards evening the Germans were back in Lwów, and hell began again.

4

THE GERMANS immediately posted orders — punishable by death — which stated that Jews had to wear arm bands bearing the Star of David, were forbidden to use public transportation, and could not be outside after curfew. They searched Jewish homes day and night, and many Jewish men were taken away and never heard from again. On one occasion, Leon wanted to hide in a cupboard when the Germans neared our apartment, but I insisted that he stand against a wall on the kitchen balcony so as not to be seen from the window when they entered. The Germans searched every cupboard and corner, but never looked out on the balcony, where we had left the door open.

A few days later, a German officer and soldiers again came to search our apartment. They ordered us to leave within the next few days and gave specific instructions as to what we were and were not allowed to take with us. We were to leave the furniture, Eva's crib and carriage, and our linens and towels. All we could take were some personal belongings. We were then told to bring the keys to the apartment to the officer at a specific address.

The following day, however, other soldiers came

to our home and ordered us to leave immediately. I tried to show them the address where I was supposed to turn in the keys in a few days, but they insisted we leave and deliver the keys that day instead. We hastily put our belongings into bundles and rushed with them to some friends nearby. My brother Levi, who was very sick with a high fever, stayed with Eva. (He had developed a subphrenic abscess of the abdomen right after the Germans returned to Lwów. I consulted some well-known physicians who came to the house, but they could not make a diagnosis before getting him into a hospital, which they promised to do. Meanwhile, the matter of leaving our apartment and finding another one was so pressing that, although he was in terrible pain, I could do nothing for him.)

A few hours later our friends informed us that they, too, had to leave their home, so we rushed with our bundles to my uncle Jacob's on the outskirts of town. When we arrived, my cousin Victor was already outside, explaining that he was on his way to tell us that they also had to leave immediately. I pleaded with a gentile Polish neighbour, who lived near my uncle and whom I knew quite well, to take our bundles until I could find a hand wagon to bring them to the centre of Lwów. While we were rushing about, we noticed that the neighbour was pulling out some of our things and hiding them in the next room for herself. Leon had to stay and watch our things while I went towards the centre of the city to find someone with a hand wagon. It did not take long, and I soon went to our place, loaded Eva's crib and the other things that were still there, and went to pick up our belongings from my uncle's neighbour.

From there we headed to the home of Moses and Adela Pohoryles. After unloading our things, we returned to the street in a panic, afraid that Leon, who looked Jewish, would be caught at any minute. An important decision had to be made: how to bring Levi to the Pohoryleses when he could hardly stand on his feet. I went out to look for a horse and carriage, but it was useless. We knew we had to leave that day because the next morning the Germans would return. We waited until it began to get dark, then Leon took Eva on his arm, covering his Star of David with her cape, and headed to the streetcar stop. Supporting my brother on my arm, we followed. Neither Levi nor I looked Jewish, and when we reached the streetcar he bought tickets for himself and for my husband. Leon remained standing with Eva on his arm, staring out of the window so that no one could see his face. They reached the stop in front of the Pohoryleses's home and managed to get Levi into the house. I returned to the apartment, loaded up Eva's carriage with as much as I could, and headed out into the darkness — without the Star of David on my arm — to our friends' place. It took me over an hour and a half, and I was exhausted after a day of no food and great physical and emotional strain. I waited for quite some time in the building until the Pohoryleses' son came to help me up with the carriage. German soldiers passed by frequently.

The next morning, I went in fear to hand in the keys to the apartment. Leon and I had decided that I had to do this, in case the German officer questioned the janitor or neighbours who might have known where we went. Although I had not left behind Eva's crib and carriage, as I had been told to do, we did not think that was as serious a crime as not handing in the keys.

The Pohoryleses lived in the centre of town, a short distance from many of the doctors. I arranged with the only Jewish surgeon left in the Jewish General Hospital (who was so good that there was no one equivalent to take his place) to bring my brother in for investigation. He and a well-known specialist in internal medicine made the diagnosis of subphrenic abscess, an abscess near the liver. Levi was in very poor condition after so many weeks of high fever, severe pain, and inadequate diet. The hospital was overcrowded and filthy. Each day when I visited Levi, he handed me a letter full of complaints and begged me to bring him back home. I was relieved, therefore, when the surgeon told me to take him home after about two weeks. Levi continued to be very ill, but all we could give him was aspirin to lower his temperature and relieve his pain.

We now lived nearer to the stores where we could sell some of our belongings to buy nourishment. On one occasion, after I had sold some things, I went to the market with quite a bit of money in my purse. After I bought some potatoes and tried to stuff them into a bag, I put my purse between my legs near my ankles, thinking that it would be easier to notice it there than under my arm if someone tried to steal it. Sure enough I soon felt a warm hand near my ankles and, grabbing the purse, I yelled out "Mama!" The man, who had been unable to grab my purse, looked at me and said in a low voice, "Be quiet or I will hit you hard," then walked slowly away. He was elegantly dressed and wore a green sporty hat with a feather in it, like a lord.

I spent a lot of time with Levi, nursing him and changing his clothes several times a day and at night, since he perspired constantly. My friends were very supportive and spent time with Eva when I was away or busy with my brother. His pain and fever gradually lessened and he began to feel slightly better. He was soon able to start eating solid foods, which consisted of black bread and potatoes.

I had told my parents about Levi's illness when he was in the hospital, since the surgeon was afraid he would not survive. They were very concerned about him, of course, and the moment we told them that he was getting better, they begged me to find a way to send him home. We tried in vain. Finally, my parents heard of some Ukrainians going by truck to Lwów. My father arranged to give one of the men a suit and a great deal more if he would bring my brother home. I packed a small suitcase and went by streetcar with a still weak Levi to meet the truck. Several Ukrainians stood around suspiciously whispering to themselves and I was extremely frightened. Levi rested on his suitcase in a yard near the truck while I tried to find out what was going on. The entire day passed. Towards evening the driver of the truck arrived and everyone climbed on. They were about to leave when I motioned to the person who was supposed to arrange my brother's transportation. She whispered something to the truck driver, who yelled back that he did not want a Jew on his truck. I went over to my brother as the truck started moving, and we dragged ourselves to a streetcar stop. When we arrived home, it was already dark. Eva was very happy to see us. Needless to say, my father never got the suit back.

Life went on. Leon and Levi hid indoors whenever people from the Jewish Council came to take men to work in the camps. I spent most of my time trying to find food to keep us alive. I was down to 95 pounds; I do not know where I got the strength or the energy to look after my child and sick brother.

I frequently ran into friends from the area where my parents lived. They told me about plans to rent a truck to return home where conditions were supposedly better and where it was easier to get food and fuel. It was late in the year by this time, and we were worried about heat for the winter. I assured my friends that they could count on the three of us and our daughter to make the trip. Meanwhile, I feverishly ran to the stores that were buying used things to sell whatever we could spare for money for the fare.

When I went into one store to sell a set of sterling silver cutlery, the owner told me that she expected a high-ranking officer at any moment who she thought would be interested in buying it. When he arrived, she took a piece from me and led him into a room at the back of the store. She soon came out with the piece of silver, telling me that he was interested in buying it but wanted to know who it was from. I grabbed the silver and ran out of the store, trying to hide in the nearest side street. When I finally slowed down I could hardly catch my breath.

The day finally came when we were to leave. We packed our belongings and went to meet the truck. There were so many people waiting to board that a number were left behind, including us. We returned home after being told by a friend that the truck would return for us in two weeks.

5

TWO WEEKS PASSED. This time, we arranged with our friend from my hometown to have the truck pick us up so that we would not have to drag our belongings back and forth if the same thing happened again. The day before we were supposed to leave, our friend assured us that everything was in order and we packed our things and prepared for the trip. We were ready before dawn. I arranged with the janitor whom I had known for many years to let the truck into the building and to close the gate while we were loading it. Eva did not like to be awakened so early and she cried a lot, causing us to fear that she would attract the attention of the Germans who were nearby. The minute I put on her coat, however, she stopped crying, since she always loved going outside. Finally, the truck was ready and we went to pick up the other people. Yet again the truck was overloaded, and when the driver tried to make room for the passengers, he put down two sacks of our clothing and then could not find space for them. He left them at the last stop with some people he knew and promised to bring them on the next trip. After several weeks he brought only one sack; the other one, containing mainly Eva's clothes, was lost.

The driver told everyone where to sit. He asked me, Eva and Levi — since we did not look Jewish — and a young gentile man from my hometown (who had come to Lwów for medical treatment and was eager to return home) to sit at the back of the truck, which was not covered by the canvas. Our journey led us through camps where we saw unfortunate young men who looked like skeletons working under the watchful eyes of German and Ukrainian guards. Late that night we reached our destination.

The people who lived near my parents' house hid in fear when they saw the truck, thinking that an "action" was taking place and that people were being collected into trucks.

My family was overjoyed to see us and all was quiet for a time. Levi went to stay with our sister Regina and I had more time to devote to Eva. After a few weeks we had all gained some weight and felt more rested after our ordeal in Lwów.

We looked around for a place of our own until we found one with some very friendly people. After a few weeks, however, the Ukrainian police confiscated it. We then searched for a new place, and moved again. The winter was severe and we had very little fuel — only enough to make a warm meal on the stove. Eva's hands were swollen from the cold all winter. She also developed chronic bronchitis and coughed so much that it was impossible for us to sleep through the night. We prayed for spring.

The awaited spring, however, was not a happy one. Rumours began to circulate that actions were going to take place to liquidate the Jewish population. A ghetto was to be formed in the largest town in the area, Borszczów. The Germans forced Jewish men to pave the sidewalks with headstones dug up from Jewish cemeteries. The names and inscriptions were placed on top for people to walk on. We discovered that if one bribed the fizyk, or public health officer, who was the chief physician of the province, it was possible to get permission to work in a large village where typhus and typhoid fever reigned, but where one was safer from the Gestapo. Leon decided to visit the public health officer in Borszczów. He brought with him a beautiful gold bracelet with three nice-sized diamonds and rubies, a gift I had previously not wanted to part with because my mother-in-law had presented it to me on my wedding day. It had been a surprise since only a few days earlier we had received a beautiful set of silver cutlery for 12 from my in-laws as a wedding gift. Leon went to Borszczów illegally, risking his life, and returned after bribing the fizyk and receiving permission to work in a large village called Dzwiniaczka, to which 17 other smaller villages belonged. He also received permission to travel between the villages and the Mielnica pharmacy, granted to him on the chief physician's request by the Jewish Council and countersigned by the Gestapo. I was relieved when Leon returned, and looked forward to an easier life in the village. I also hoped that Eva's bronchitis would improve in the warmer weather.

Shortly after that, we went to Dzwiniaczka to look for a place to live. We had no transportation, so we left Eva with relatives and set out on foot. We were tired when we arrived, but immediately went to the village hall to present our permission to work and to ask the mayor to help us find a place to live. He helped us find a large house on the largest farm in the village, which we shared with the landlady. We were not as successful in finding transportation back, though, and had to walk home. When we arrived it was almost dark. We found a man with a horse and buggy and after my father helped us pack and load our possessions, we went off to the village. We arrived on a beautiful spring day and settled in with the help of our landlady, her family, and neighbours. They were friendlier toward us than were the Ukrainian and Polish people in the town.

The house had a large courtyard, a garden, and barns with cows, horses and chickens. The landlady's grandchild was Eva's age, and the two children explored and played together. Patients started to come to us almost immediately since there had been no other doctors in the village. After a few weeks, the mayors of each of the 17 villages had received a supply of vaccines against typhoid fever, and had sent a horse and buggy for us to administer them. We were immediately inoculating thousands of people day in and day out. We brought Eva, who was two and a half years old at the time, along with us, since we never knew what might happen and didn't want to risk being separated from her.

We worked hard, travelling between the villages, but felt relatively at peace. Patients paid for our visits with a loaf of bread, some flour or potatoes; we were never hungry. About once a week when we went to Mielnica, I brought food to my parents and sisters. My mother, in her good-heartedness, used to tell me that she shared the little bit of food she had for herself and my father with some poor people who depended on people like her to stay alive. And so the summer of 1942 passed in relative quiet.

Toward the end of the summer, however, a big action occurred in Mielnica in which hundreds of Jews were suddenly caught and transported in freight and cattle wagons so crowded that some suffocated and died standing, according to witnesses who escaped. No one knew where they were taken. My family, miraculously, was the only one in town that remained intact. My father made a hiding place in the chimney in a dilapidated home nearby. He took one of my brothers-in-law, Isidore, and a grandson, Markus, with him, since only three people could fit in the chimney. Three women neighbours ran into my parents' home and my mother led them down to the cellar under the kitchen floor, closed the back door and covered it with a rag, and put a piece of furniture on top. She then went up to the attic, into the farthest corner under the roof, and covered herself with a large carton containing my sister's wedding gown. She heard the Gestapo and Ukrainian police enter the house, and then the voices of the Ukrainian neighbours identifying the entrance through the kitchen floor to the cellar. In a few minutes the police brought the three women up, screaming, and led them away. The Gestapo then came up to search the attic, very near to where my mother was hiding, but did not suspect that anyone could be hiding under the box since it was so small.

Everyone stayed in their hiding places until it was completely dark and quiet. My oldest sister, Lottie, then took her daughter, Eva, and ran to hide in the fields, where they were safe. (Her husband was taken by the Soviets to Siberia because he was considered a bourgeois.) My other two sisters, Rachel and Regina, with their sons, Philip and Julek, and my brother-in-law, Baruch, also managed to escape to safety in the fields. My brother, Levi, who worked for a Ukrainian cooperative at a nearby village near the train station, received word about the action and hid in one of the warehouses. A Polish pedlar came to our village and told us what was going on in the town. We immediately took off by foot to another village, where we stayed for a short time with some patients we had befriended.

Immediately after the action ended, hundreds of Poles and Ukrainians rushed into town with horses and buggies. They took all the possessions left by the Jews who were taken away, including the doors, windows, and whatever else they could find. The Jewish part of town was converted into ruins.

A few weeks later, we had a terrible encounter. Fall had set in and we had begun to think about fuel for the winter. I went to see a forester, a Polish man our landlady told me was selling wood in exchange for merchandise (probably illegally). At first he seemed uninterested in anything I had to offer him: shirts, suits, dresses, and the like. I finally offered him two pieces of material that Leon and I had received with our trousseau to make suits, but had never used. The Pole insisted that he wanted to see the fabrics before we made a deal. He came to our place the next day to see the samples I had prepared for him, but still refused to strike a bargain, claiming that he needed time to think about what to offer us in return.

Weeks passed and he did not return. When I went to his home I was told he was not there. On one of our trips into town, we ended up selling a piece of the material to a Jewish man who probably traded it for food. We kept the other piece under some linens in the cupboard. I don't know why, but the next day after we returned from town I took the piece of material out of the cupboard and hid it under the straw mattress on our bed. A few hours later the forester appeared with a German border policeman (Grenzschutz) who, without saying a word, began to violently beat Leon. He hit him again and again with the butt of his rifle, repeatedly striking him on the head, face, and neck. My husband was covered with blood. The veins on his neck were so engorged that I was afraid they would explode. Eva held on to me, crying, while I yelled out, "What do you want from us?" The policeman retorted, "Don't talk or I will hit you too. Give me the two pieces of material," and held out the samples. I told him I had no material. I knew that he would never be satisfied with just the one piece of cloth, and I was afraid he would torture us until we produced the second. I could not let him know which Jew had bought the first piece because this meant certain death for him; business deals were not allowed. The policeman ordered us to sit on top of a table while he searched our apartment.

The first place he looked was the cupboard where the material had been. He then opened a suitcase filled with dirty laundry. He didn't want to touch it himself so he told us to come down from the table to take it out. He then walked over to the bed. I immediately pulled the sheet up to cover the material. Suddenly, Eva let go of my hand and I found myself — as if transported in air — removing the material and taking it through the door that was near the kitchen out into the hall and down the stairs and into the yard and then into a potato storage shack where I hid it deep among some dried up potato stems and leaves. Amazingly, no one saw me do it. My daughter remained standing where I had left her. Neither the policeman nor the forester nor the dozens of people working in the yard for the harvest noticed anything. Only my husband saw what I had done, and he gave me a look of despair that clearly indicated we were lost.

I returned to my place in the room and Eva took my hand. The German border policeman was still searching through the straw in the mattress and had not noticed anything. Finally, the policeman and the forester went out of the house and asked Leon to follow them. Eva and I trailed closely behind. There was a carriage waiting. The policeman and the forester got in and sat down, facing backwards, and told my husband to run behind them as fast as they drove. Otherwise, the policeman said, pointing to the gun in his hand, he would shoot him. I do not know where Leon got the strength to run as fast as he did after the beating he had suffered. Eva and I could not keep up, of course, and we quickly lost sight of him. I desperately asked everyone we passed to tell me if they saw in which direction the carriage and Leon had gone. At last someone said that they had driven into the yard where the border police were stationed. When we arrived Leon was on his way out. He could hardly hold himself up, and he could not speak. His neck and face were swollen and bloody. I used all my strength to support him and Eva, who was also holding on to me. When we were outside the gate, a woman who had witnessed the incident told me that she would rather have seen my husband shot to death than beaten so badly. We dragged ourselves home very slowly; it was a long distance. I washed the blood off Leon's head and put compresses on his face and neck. He was unable to even whisper for a few days and his voice remained hoarse for many weeks. During the first week I fed him milk from a teaspoon. (Our landlady had previously refused to sell us milk, claiming she did not have enough.) Slowly he recovered.

A few weeks later the same border policeman came to our village, went to the Ukrainian police, and expressed his desire to "finish up" my husband. An official from the mayor's office who was at the police station at the time — and whom we later discovered to be Jewish — came to inform us of the border policeman's intentions. Leon's first reaction was to leave immediately, and I agreed. He rushed down the street and Eva and I went to a neighbour's house. I asked her to hide us, since night had set in. My landlady knew where we were and a little while later her daughter came to tell us that the border policeman and Ukrainian police were there searching for us. The landlady tried hard to dissuade them from breaking in, assuring them that we were not there, but it was no use. Our neighbour became frightened when she heard this and asked me to leave, saying that she would agree only to keep Eva. I tried to quickly explain to my daughter that I would return, but she cried bitterly as I left. The neighbour locked the door behind me.

I went out into the darkness and crawled between some thick bushes near the house. I couldn't decide whether to stay or to go, to leave my crying child or to risk taking her with me. A few minutes later I heard the policemen approaching and saw the lights from their flashlights. I stayed very still. They searched all through the gardens and around the houses and barns. Eva must have fallen asleep because she suddenly quieted down. After some time it appeared that the police had left, but I remained crouched in the bushes until morning. I then took Eva and went to another neighbour's house across the street. I still had no idea where Leon was.

During the next few days Eva and I went from one neighbour's house to another, afraid to return home. I finally sent someone to ask my landlady if she had heard from Leon. It turned out that she had, a few days earlier. I quickly sent word to him to stay where he was for another few days while I returned home first. When he finally joined us, he said that he had spent the first night in a field where stray dogs had barked at him and he had been afraid he would be bitten.

The same border policeman returned alone one night a few weeks later. We knew that this might occur and had prepared ourselves. There was a window in our bedroom leading out to an orchard. Leon was tall and could easily jump out of this window, so whenever we heard the slightest knock or sound he would do so. I would hand him Eva, who by now was trained to keep completely quiet at such times, and then he would help me down. We had prepared a piece of board to hold the window closed once we were down. (The window was on the opposite side of the entrance door.) Once we were certain that no one was on that side of the house, we would run down to the orchard, escaping through a board in the fence that we had prepared. This was held in place with a stone once we were on the other side. From there we would run into the fields to hide in ditches or with people we knew.

We had a few incidents with the German border police that fall. One of them came into our kitchen one evening, his breath smelling strongly of alcohol, and ordered Leon to take Eva and leave the house. Then he asked me to go to bed with him, graphically describing his sexual preferences. I took the kerosene lamp from the kitchen table and pretended to lead him into the bedroom. On the way there, I blew out the lamp, put it down, and ran out the other door. I hid in the potato shack. Leon alerted the landlady, an elderly woman, to be on the lookout. After some time, the drunken policeman found his way out of the dark house and, unable to hold himself up, fell into a ditch in front of the house. The landlady helped him out and directed him to the road. For several days we wandered around, afraid to return home.

Another incident with the Gestapo also ended in a close call. All farmers were supposed to report to the mayor the amount of crops they brought home and the number of livestock they possessed. A German was assigned to decide what portion was to be given to the Germans — which was the majority — and what small part they could keep for themselves. Many farmers, however, hid what they could before reporting. One farmer killed a pig without permission and hid the meat in some grain. He had a fight with his wife who reported him to the border police (Grenzschutz), who in turn reported it to the Gestapo. The Gestapo came and ripped the skin off the man's chest and back, tearing his muscles and exposing his ribs. He was then made to show them the hiding place. As soon as the Gestapo left, a neighbour ran to get Leon to attend to the wounded man, not telling him what had happened. On their way there the Gestapo came across them, stopped Leon, and asked where he was going. He told them and showed them the permission papers signed by the Gestapo from Borszczów. To this one of them said, "The man has no bad intentions; he wears his arm band." I had been walking with Eva some distance behind my husband. When the Gestapo approached him, we hid behind a fence and watched to see what would happen, but they let him go a few minutes later. Some villagers also watched the incident and told me afterwards that they had never heard of such a case: a Jew had encountered the Gestapo and had walked away without even being touched.

We used to hide from time to time in a nearby convent where the nuns were quite nice to us and asked us to come to them when there was an urgent need. After being there for a day or two a few times, the Sister Superior suggested that we leave our daughter with them so she would grow up "on the bosom of the real God." We then realized what lay behind their hospitable behaviour.

The severe winter set in. Leon travelled a lot between villages since there were so many sick people. They paid very little — usually just with a loaf of bread or a small bag of potatoes — but it meant a lot to us. He also managed to get some kerosene for our lamp so that we were not left in the dark at night, as well as some wood for our stove to make a warm meal and to heat the house. I mostly stayed at home with Eva since it was so cold. Occasionally Leon was unable to return from his trips because of snowstorms or other reasons, and I spent the night worrying about him. Usually on such occasions, I rose early and left my sleeping daughter with the landlady while I set out on foot for miles until I met him.

The Germans were somewhat quieter that winter; they were unaccustomed to the severe cold and it limited their activities. We had a few more scares, however, and had to leave home for several days at a time. It was difficult to walk in the deep snow carrying Eva through the fields. We never took the main roads for fear of encountering the Germans. From time to time we went to town to see my family and to bring them food. They managed somehow to get some fuel, and to continue their miserable existence through the winter. We received letters from Leon's family and sent them packages of bread and a little money; that was all we could do for them.

During the winter we also received letters from the Pohoryleses, with whom I had stayed in Lwów during my high school years, and from my friends the Chazins in whose home we had had our wedding. We sent them also a few small parcels of bread, oil, beans and the like. We became friendly with a

Ukrainian priest in a nearby village who had a radio. All radios were supposed to be turned in when the Germans arrived. For Jews, failure to obey meant certain death; for Gentiles, a harsh penalty but not as severe. Our landlady told us that the priest, in his sermons, used to point out the heavenly rewards for giving persecuted people shelter and sharing with them their daily bread. Yet in the next village another Ukrainian priest agitated the entire community by asking his parishioners to denounce any Jew they knew because all Jews were Christ-killers. Upon hearing this, we left our home for several days.

During the winter, our friend the priest brought us the news that the Germans were doing poorly on the Russian front and had to retreat in several places. He later told us that the Germans were losing on all sides of the front. We hoped and prayed that they would lose the war soon, and that we would finally be free. The priest had heard of a speech by one of the German generals who said that they were disadvantaged because of the severe temperatures, but that once spring arrived they would advance to Moscow.

By mid-February, warm weather had set in, the snow had mostly melted, and the road and hilly parts of the ground around the house were completely dry. When I walked around and saw the thaw, anger revolted in me to such an extent that I felt severe pressure, like a pain, in my chest. Sure enough, the Germans started to advance once again.

Late in the spring, a rumour started to circulate that a ghetto would be formed in Borszczów. We went to town frequently to find out more: we knew that we would not be allowed to remain in the village once the order came out to go to the ghetto. We always left Eva with a neighbour since we never knew what would happen in town and it would be more difficult to run or hide with a child. By then she had been trained to stay in any strange place alone.

The wife of the Ukrainian police chief was a patient of Leon's, and we tried to win him over to our side. We told him that we would probably have to go to Borszczów soon and would lose our possessions, so we preferred to give them to him. He eagerly agreed and came back that evening with his wife to collect whatever was not hidden, including the towels we were using. He promised us that no matter what kind of denunciations there would be against us, he would never send his men after us. He was a gypsy, a Ukrainian, a vagrant and a known murderer, but he kept his promise to us. As long as we were in our place in the village, he used to come frequently to bring us news and to call us "my friend." He had spent some time in Czechoslovakia as a boy and had learned the language and liked to converse with us in Czech. Mostly he came to visit us in the evenings, and when Leon was not home he shook hands with me, showing his shining white teeth, and a shiver of fear would shoot through me. However, I always tried to keep a pleasant expression on my face and offered him a drink, which we kept exclusively for him.

6

THE RUMOURS INCREASED that Jews would soon be ordered to go to the ghetto. We were told by the chief of police in our village that there would probably be a big action in Borszczów after the Jews were gathered there. We debated what to do: to concentrate on going to the ghetto or on finding a hiding place. Leon, during his travels between villages, had approached different people whom he considered relatively reliable to ask them to hide us. The majority refused, legitimately pointing out that it would mean risking their own lives. Others said that they would hide us but not Eva, since they did not believe she could stay quiet. Still others advised us to hide the child with a large family with children about her own age.

We decided first to find a place for Eva. Since her mother tongue was Polish, it had to be a Polish family. Many of the people we asked refused to take her, saying that with her blond, fair looks she resembled a little countess compared to their children, and that the neighbours would immediately notice her and report her to the police. After quite some time, we found a Polish teacher who had three children of her own who was willing to take in Eva. She and Leon agreed to let a rumour circulate that the teacher's sister, who lived in a distant city, was sending her daughter because she herself was too sick to look after her. Allegedly, someone from this area would bring the child to the train station for the teacher to pick up. She would then pick up Eva instead and bring her home. The teacher was supposed to come to our house to meet Eva and to discuss financial conditions. Meanwhile, we explained to our daughter that an aunt by the name of Sławka was coming to visit, and that she would take her home to play with her three children, Eva's cousins. Eva gradually became used to the idea, and appeared to be ready to go. I packed her belongings, along with a half sack of flour, potatoes, and whatever else I could find of worth in the house.

Meanwhile, Leon decided to go to town to see my family, who were preparing to go to the ghetto. When he told them that we had found a place for Eva and that she was to be picked up the next day, they expressed their disapproval. My sister Rachel was especially opposed, insisting that the child would be lonely and if the neighbours reported her, it would be terrible for us to survive if she perished. We reconsidered and decided that whatever might happen, we would stick together. We sent word to the teacher telling her that we had changed our minds.

A few days later, we found out that there was hardly a Jewish soul remaining in town; all but one other family had been forced to leave under threat of death. The family that remained consisted of a Jewish doctor and his wife and child. We agreed with them that whoever found out first that it was time to disappear should let the other family know.

We decided to go to Borszczów to ask the chief physician's advice. We left Eva with the landlady and took off by horse and buggy with valuable gifts. We spent the night with my parents, my older sister and her children, and my brother, who lived together in a small apartment. My father found a place for the driver and carriage. In the morning, we went to see the chief physician, who advised us to stay and continue functioning as we had been since he had not been asked to revoke our permission papers and there was no general announcement to the contrary in the village. Of course, there was also no assurance that the Gestapo would not come directly to us and order us to go to the ghetto — or shoot us on the spot.

I realized then how right my sister had been in regard to leaving our daughter. After we returned from Borszczów, our landlady told us that although Eva was very much at home with her and her family — we had been living there for a year and a half — she cried for us at night, refusing to eat or to get undressed. She sat on the bed until midnight when she finally fell asleep. Her shoes were taken off while she was sleeping but when she woke again she asked for them, and held them tightly while she slept. Her happiness when she saw us that day was indescribable.

We continued to live in great fear during the summer of 1943. We were the only Jews left within a very large area. The slightest sound or knock on the door terrified us, and we did not go to town any more because we were so afraid. In any case, my family was no longer there.

Rumours persisted of a big action in Borszczów. We decided to bring my parents to us, believing that young people might manage to escape on their own but the old ones would definitely perish. We went to a villager who had a horse and buggy and offered him money and clothes to go and bring my parents. He had no use for the clothes since almost all Ukrainians in the area wore the national costumes that they wove and made themselves. However, he said that he needed a hat so Leon gave him one and we agreed on the money we were to give him after he brought my parents. He was to leave early in the morning and bring my parents to us in the evening. We waited until midnight that day but there was no sign of the villager or my parents. Leon went to the driver's home to find out if he had returned, but the house was dark and a large, vicious dog was barking loudly. No one came out of the house. When Leon returned we decided that if my parents didn't arrive during the night we would have to go back to the villager's house early the next morning before he could leave his home. I sat near the window all night watching for them.

Early the next morning we left our sleeping daughter with the landlady and went to find the villager. The dog was still outside, running loose and barking, when the villager came out. He told us that he had gone to my parents and arranged with them when and where to meet. On his way home, he had met a close acquaintance who insisted he take him and his family to the area where we were living. Therefore, there was no room for my parents. He tried to assure us, however, that he would go again soon to get them.

When we returned from the villager's, our landlady told us that she had heard that the Ukrainian police had been called to Borszczów during the night because something clearly was going to happen there. Since my brother Levi worked in Borszczów for a Ukrainian cooperative, I decided to call him when the post office opened at nine o'clock. (One could only make phone calls from the post office.) Meanwhile, Leon went to Mielnica to try to find out what the Jewish doctor there was planning to do.

He managed to get a horse and buggy and left as soon as he could. We were under tremendous tension. I left Eva with the landlady and went to the post office early. Jews were not allowed to make phone calls, but the postmaster did us a favour since he needed help from us for his family from time to time. It took a long time to make the connection because he had to wait until no one was around when he let me into the phone booth. When I finally got hold of one of the men from the cooperative and asked for my brother, the man replied, "Kimmel went into the other world." I could not and did not believe what he said and kept repeating, "That is not possible. How do you know?" The man assured me that he knew positively that my brother had been shot that morning and that the action was still going on. For a moment I felt faint and could hardly hold myself up. A rage began to build inside me, causing tremendous pain and pressure until I thought my chest would burst. I could not stay still or walk normally; I had to run. And so I ran, crying, from the post office all the way into town and to the doctor's home where I found Leon and poured out my terrible grief. Nothing that he, the doctor, or his wife said could even begin to relieve my pain. To this day, I cannot understand why my brother did not hide in the warehouses as he had done before. Was he prevented from doing so by the men in the cooperative? He was a quiet, considerate person, well-liked by the other workers. Was he trying to send off my parents and could not get back there in time?

Some of the villagers told us that they had seen the Ukrainian police coming back from the action in

Borszczów and that as they passed the church they crossed themselves. Others told us that soon after their return they boasted about how many Jews they had killed.

We found out a short while later that the same day the villager had seen my parents there had been a tremendous panic in Borszczów. Because the Ukrainian police had gathered there from all over, it was almost certain that the big action would occur the next day. People desperately looked for ways to leave the city. The villager had been offered a great deal more money from other people than he had from us so he took them instead of my parents. We were told that my parents were seen waiting for the villager near the road where they had agreed to meet him, but that when it grew dark they returned to the city, afraid to be on the street after curfew.

The terrible action took place the next day. My parents, together with my beloved younger brother who had just recovered from his lengthy illness, were caught and killed. From a Jew in the Jewish Council we knew that when people were caught, they were gathered together in a certain spot where some were assigned to dig a huge grave and then all were shot near the edge of it so that most fell in. On the way to this spot people were forced to undress and parade naked, sometimes ordered to sing or do exercises. My father, who had a very strong character, declared after they found him that he wanted to be shot on the spot. He insisted that no one would make a fool of him. While he was being beaten and forced to leave the house he held onto the door frame and the Gestapo could not tear him away. He was beaten over the head with the butt of a rifle until his skull burst and his brains splattered out. My mother and brother had to look on. My brother could not control himself and told the Gestapo that they knew as well as he did that they would lose the war soon and that by being so brutal they were only doing more harm to themselves. The day after the action my sister came back to the house and found my father in that state at the door.

My mother and brother were dragged naked to the central place where, as punishment, my brother had to dig a grave while my mother looked on, not only watching her beloved youngest son dig his own grave but also being shot before her eyes. Then she too was shot.

7

AFTER THE DEATH of my parents and brother, I became seriously depressed. I was unable to take care of anyone, including my child. Eva spent most of her time with our landlady and her family, who fed her when they had their meals. Otherwise, Leon looked after her, although he was preoccupied with where we would go next, since we knew that we couldn't remain in our place much longer. Our landlady and her family accused me of being a martyr, since I frequently expressed feelings of guilt over not finding a more reliable villager to bring my parents to us. Had I indirectly hastened their deaths?

A few days later the Polish peddler who used to visit our landlady came to our place and told us that he was surprised to still see us there. Apparently, the doctor from the town and his family had disappeared a few days previously after hearing that all the doctors in the neighbouring small towns had been shot by the Gestapo. We immediately closed up our place and left. We walked through the fields into the next village where we knew a wealthy and reliable farmer by the name of Kukurudza. His son was sick with tuberculosis of the bones and had been treated by Leon for some time. The treatment at that time consisted of calcium injections, and Leon travelled frequently to give them to him. We knew that Kukurudza would try to keep us close by so that Leon could continue to treat his son, saving them from travelling an entire day by horse and buggy to see the doctor in town. He would also have to pay for those visits properly — not just with a loaf of bread or a few eggs, as he did with my husband.

Kukurudza, however, was afraid to let us stay with him, just as we were afraid to do so for fear that people in the village would recognize us. We asked him to find us a safe place to stay for a few days while we looked for a reliable person to build a bunker for us. We then asked him to go back to our place with us by horse and buggy to collect our belongings. He agreed to do this, and as soon as it got dark we left Eva with his wife and went back to our place. When we returned, we sorted and repacked our things into suitcases and wooden boxes. Kukurudza was afraid to keep our things in his home, in case of a search, so he dug a hole in the stable, buried our things, and covered them with soil and straw. We were very concerned about our belongings because we knew that as long as we had something to trade or to give for our upkeep, we might remain alive. Once we no longer possessed anything, no one would keep us for even a day. For the rest of that night, Kukurudza put us up in the furthest shack from the house, which was a pigsty, since he was afraid there might be a search for us the next morning. If we heard anything during the night, we could run from the pigsty into the fields. The smell and squeaking of the pigs were almost unbearable, but we spent a few days there since Kukurudza could find no other place for us. Finally, a trusted neighbour agreed to take us in for a few nights, deciding that the safest place for us would be to sit in his chimney. We almost suffocated from smoke, but at least there were no pigs.

Kukurudza heard about Jews who had run away from Borszczów, reached the outskirts of our village, and then been shot by the Ukrainian police. He got scared and decided that when it got dark he would take us out into the fields most distant from his house, where he thought we would be safer. We took a small pillow for Eva, an umbrella, a large pitcher of water and some food and set off. Leon carried Eva and I took all the other things. Kukurudza walked far ahead of us so that he could hide in a ditch or in the fields if we were caught. Avoiding the road, we walked mainly through orchards, sometimes passing very close to houses. At one point we got very scared when Eva cried out loudly after her bonnet got caught on a tree branch and was pulled off her head. In general, she was well-trained not to cry or say anything — even if dogs were barking or jumping at us. We could see people in a house through the window and we ran as fast as we could until we reached the fields. We cleared a spot in the tall wheat. The air seemed clean and all was quiet.

Kukurudza promised to bring us food and water the next evening. We felt safe, slept well, and woke refreshed after so many difficult sleepless nights. However, this feeling of well-being did not last long. People were working in nearby fields and we could not even stand up without being noticed. We had to sit in the clearing we had made for ourselves and talk in whispers. The sun was soon so hot that we were literally gasping for air. We were also perspiring profusely, but we had very little water left and could not use any of it since Eva demanded water constantly. When Kukurudza returned that night we told him how difficult the day had been and asked him if he had had a chance to look for a place for us. He assured us that it was constantly on his mind, but since it was so important to maintain secrecy, it was not easy for him to approach just anybody. He brought us more water and food.

The next day was even hotter and more humid than the previous one. We tried without success to cover our heads with whatever we could find. There was not even a breeze in the wheat. Towards evening there was a tremendous thunder and lightning storm. There is a difference between witnessing such a storm from the safety of one's home and being in the middle of a field. I had never before been afraid of a storm, but I was now. We crouched down on the ground, shielding Eva between us with the umbrella. We were soaking wet but she remained dry. When the rain eased Kukurudza returned. He told us that it would probably rain all night and that he would take us to his place for the night and possibly the next day, but we would have to return to the field the next evening. We left the pillow and blanket folded under the umbrella, secured it with a stone, and followed him.

The next morning a cow happened to escape into the fields and its owner, a woman, followed her until they reached our spot. She immediately realized who was hiding there, took our belongings, and spread the news around the village. We were all very frightened and Kukurudza, out of desperation, approached the mayor of the village who was a good friend of his. The mayor agreed to let us stay in his shack for a few days and promised to try to find someone in the village to take us in. We were hopeful, since we knew that he had a lot of influence on people. He even apologized for making us stay in the shack, explaining that many people came to his house, including the police, and it would be too dangerous for us to stay there. He also went to the woman who was spreading gossip about our hiding in Kukurudza's field, chastised her for taking our belongings, and warned her to keep quiet. We were nervous about that, as well, since we didn't know what the woman's reaction might be.

For the next two days neither Kukurudza nor anyone from the mayor's family appeared at our shack. We were all very hungry. Whenever Eva asked for something to eat, we would first look around carefully to see if anyone was watching, then Leon would go out to a nearby apple tree, tear off an unripe apple or two, and run back. I fed Eva pieces of the apple until I was near the core, then Leon would quickly say "Give it to me." Eva immediately developed severe diarrhoea. We could do nothing but constantly peer out through a crack in the door to try to attract the mayor's attention. Finally we spotted his daughter and called her over to ask her to let Kukurudza know that we needed some food.

One evening Kukurudza came by and said that he thought the field watchman of the village would agree to take us in. His name was Krawczuk, a very poor man with a wife and three children, and for money or clothing he might be willing to risk building a bunker for us. Kukurudza did not think Krawczuk would denounce us, but he planned to have the mayor speak to him before anything was agreed upon.

We were very anxious to find a place for a longer period of time, especially since Krawczuk might be willing to build a bunker for us. We told Kukurudza to assure him that we would try to give him as much as we could. A couple of days later Kukurudza came to bring us to him.

At first we had to stay in the attic over his house. Krawczuk's wife brought us food twice a day, in the morning and in the late afternoon. She prepared mostly warm meals, like soup, which were very important to us, and especially for Eva. (We had previously subsisted on coarse bread and a lukewarm tea brewed from herbs.) Sometimes we had fruit when it was in season. Each time, after using the stepladder to the attic, the woman locked it up in the pantry so that her children, who did not know we were there, could not go up.

One morning after we had been there for a few days we heard a lot of commotion. We peeked through a hole in the straw roof and saw people running toward the house. The roof was on fire! It had started in the back of the house and was spreading rapidly. We crouched down near the entrance to the attic but the stepladder was not there. People were running in and out of the house, but there was no sign of the field watchman or his wife. As the smoke started to choke us, we debated what to do: I thought that Leon should jump down first, take Eva from me, and then help me down. However, he was afraid that it was too high a jump and we would probably get hurt and attract attention to ourselves. We were convinced that this was our end — either we would burn to death, hurt ourselves by jumping, or be denounced by the people. At the last minute, just as we were about to make a decision, Krawczuk's wife appeared and yelled at everyone to go to the back of the house where the fire most needed to be extinguished. She handed out pails to bring water from the well, which was on the side of the house. After quickly checking to make sure that no one was watching, she then put up the stepladder and we ran down into the pantry. She locked us up together with the stepladder.

The fire was quickly extinguished and the crowd slowly dispersed. We remained worried, however, since we were not sure whether or not anyone had noticed us. If they had, it would mean that we would surely be denounced — or lose our new haven and be forced to wander about again from place to place.

We stayed in the pantry until dark, at which time Krawczuk brought us to the attic over the stable. The air was bad there, but we were used to such conditions by then. He told us that it would take quite some time to build a new roof for the house.

8

A FEW DAYS PASSED and all seemed relatively peaceful. Krawczuk brought home freshly-ripened potatoes, corn, beans, and peas and his wife cooked them and brought us plenty to eat.

It was about this time that my only remaining sister, Rachel, sent us a message through our previous landlady that she and her husband and son were hiding in some woods near the train station. From time to time they would risk their lives by going into the village for food. She asked me to try to help them. I was shocked to receive her letter; I had been sure that she and her son were no longer alive, since during the last days of our stay in Dzwiniaczka a man from the village had gone to Borszczów and brought me a letter from my brother-in-law in which he lamented their deaths. Our previous landlady did not know where we were, but she sensed that if anyone knew of our whereabouts it would be Kukurudza. She gave him my sister's message. Kukurudza then asked the landlady to spread the rumour that while trying to cross the border to Rumania, we had all been shot. Almost immediately our current landlady came to us with news of the rumour, which had quickly spread between villages. She was glad there would be no suspicion.

After Kukurudza gave us Rachel's message, I immediately asked him to take some of our own flour for his wife to bake bread. I then asked him to give it to the man who had brought the message from my sister and ask him to forward it to her. I felt justified in asking these favours — for which he was paid — since all along, no matter where we were, when it was time for his son's injections he still got Leon to administer them. He would take him at night and sneak him back through orchards and fields. Leon was able to secure the calcium he needed for the injections from a pharmacist friend.

I also told Kukurudza that I would talk to the field watchman about taking in Rachel and her family. When I told Krawczuk that he would be paid for keeping the three members of my sister's family as well as for us, he said he was willing to give it a try. Before Kukurudza left I asked him to leave a message with Rachel's contact that he would come on foot on a certain night and bring them to us. Naturally, we promised to pay him well for this, too.

A few days later Kukurudza went to get my sister and her son, Philip. It was so far away that he did not return before daylight. Finally, he came over to tell us that they were safely in his home, and that in a few days he would return for my brother-in-law, Baruch, since he had been afraid to bring everyone at once. I would have to wait until then to see them.

I was so anxious to see Rachel and to learn what had happened to the rest of our family that I simply could not wait for Kukurudza to return with Baruch. I begged him to let me come over early the next morning, before it was light, to spend the day with my sister and nephew. He reluctantly agreed. I brought Eva with me because after being together constantly for so many months, I was afraid to leave her behind.

We reached Kukurudza's safely the next morning and climbed up to the attic. However, we had little chance to talk. When we arrived, Rachel and Philip were still sound asleep, exhausted from their long walk. Almost as soon as they awoke, Kukurudza's wife came running to warn us to be quiet since something had happened at a neighbour's house and the Ukrainian police were nearby. Though we were all very frightened, I was taken by surprise when Rachel said she wanted to take Philip and hide. I didn't say anything at the time, but I was astonished that she would want to hide alone, with only her son, after I had risked so much for her and had been so eager for us to be together. For the rest of the day we sat quietly apart, hidden in hay. I was glad when it got dark and Kukurudza came to bring us back to our attic. When we returned, Leon told me that it had been a very difficult day for him, too, and that he did not think he could continue hiding if he were alone.

A few days later, Rachel and her family came to

live in the attic over Krawczuk's house. We thought it would be easier to keep the children quiet if we were apart, so we remained in the attic over the stable. At night when the children were asleep, Krawczuk, Rachel, and Baruch would come over to discuss how and where to build a bunker, since fall was approaching and nights in the attic were cold. The ground behind the house was very hilly and above, on a plain, was an orchard. Two small doors on the elevation were visible from the house. One of them led to a potato storage area that was quite deep and had stone-covered walls and a stone ceiling. The other door led to a chicken coop on the same level as the house. It was quite low and had earthen walls and floor. We decided to take some of the stones out of the wall of the potato cellar in the direction of the chicken coop so that the six of us could have room to lie down. There would be an opening in the floor of the chicken coop, leading to our bunker, which would be hidden by a chicken feeder, a dish with many small holes and some corn. We could breathe through the chicken coop, but the air was unbearably nauseating.

Our idea was easier said than done. As soon as it got dark and the neighbours went inside, Krawczuk, Leon, and Baruch started to dig out the bunker. The other two women and I left the sleeping children and hauled pails of soil into the vegetable garden. We tried to flatten the earth with a shovel so that it would not appear suspicious to the neighbours. After weeks of strenuous digging, the weather got so cold that we had to move into the bunker. Krawczuk brought us some straw and the six of us huddled together, almost one on top of the other, covered with our coats. We no longer had any blankets or covers. During the day we burned oil in a hollowed potato with a wick in it for light. Krawczuk's wife came twice a day with food, which was becoming increasingly scarce now that the produce was being taken directly from the fields and her husband had little to bring home. He was afraid to start buying food since he had never done so before and did not want to raise suspicion. On the other hand, his wife altered clothes that I had given her and wore them to church. They were much nicer than her own clothes, and we were very concerned that this would attract attention. I am convinced that the reason the police never paid attention to any rumours about us was because the chief of police had kept his promise.

Since we had left home we rarely had a chance to wash, change clothes, or undress for the night, and we soon became infested with lice. I tried everything I could to get rid of them. The biting was annoying to us all. In the bunker, it was even worse; none of us could sleep because of our constant scratching. Rachel and I would sit near the crack of the little door in the potato cellar and search our clothing for lice, dumping them into bottles of water. They seemed to be able to swim! We disposed of them when the pail of waste was taken out. We also got head lice and I eventually had to cut off Eva's beautiful hair, since her scalp was full of sores and she cried whenever I tried to comb her hair. We also had mice, rats, and lizards. When we kept bread for more than a few hours — which was rare — we had to make sure it was well-protected.

During quiet moments, three of us would go into the potato cellar for a glimpse of daylight through the slit in the door. On sunny days, when a ray of sun could be seen, Eva was always impressed, exclaiming, "Mummy, I saw the sun!" Occasionally, we would also go into the potato cellar to use an empty pail we kept for our needs, and a pail of water for bathing.

Leon continued giving injections to Kukurudza's son. Every so often he would return with some milk or a few boiled eggs — a rare treat for the children. Sometimes he and Kukurudza would have to stop and hide for a while until they could continue without being seen. On such occasions I always became extremely worried, afraid that something terrible had happened to him. I remember once when Leon did not return all night; he and the farmer had come across someone on their way and had been forced to take a much more roundabout route home.

And so the winter passed. We routinely asked Kukurudza to unearth some of the things that we had hidden — like the set of silver cutlery that had been a gift from my in-laws, the silver candelabra from my parents, and our sheets, linens, and tablecloths — to pay off the field watchman. Kukurudza would sell our things for a fraction of their worth to Ukrainians from a cooperative in a distant village. The cooperative was the only place we knew of that would always buy the things we sent with the farmer. They knew where the things came from, but we were quite sure they were not the type of people who would denounce us.

A few months later we heard of one or two cases in which Jews were discovered in bunkers and had been shot together with the person who hid them. Krawczuk became understandably frightened and asked us to find another place to hide. We tried to explain to him that leaving the bunker in the middle of the winter would mean certain death for us, since the fields were bare and we would freeze to death even if we were lucky enough to find another attic to stay in. Eva liked Krawczuk very much and when she heard us pleading she spoke up, telling him she loved him so that he would not ask us to leave. She always called him "uncle" and would run to sit on his lap when he came into the bunker. Krawczuk replied that it was only because of Eva that he had not asked us to leave sooner.

9

KRAWCZUK BECAME increasingly nervous about hiding us and continued to bring up the subject of our leaving. At the same time he reproached us for entrusting ourselves — but not our possessions — to him. It was true; for those, we had more confidence in Kukurudza. Our relationship with the field watchman became more and more strained, our possessions grew fewer, food became extremely poor, and the end of winter was still far from sight. To add to our difficulties, Eva developed severe diarrhoea and a high fever that lasted for weeks. Her abdomen was so huge that when she tried to sit up she said, "My tummy does not let me sit up." When we asked Krawczuk for boiled water for her, he replied, "Don't worry. Despite the winter, I will bury her in the garden when she dies."

One day in March 1944, as our desperation mounted, Krawczuk told us that he had heard there had been constant shooting and the Soviets apparently had the upper hand; the Germans were retreating on the front. We hoped and prayed this was true. A few days later we could also hear the shooting, and saw all sorts of vehicles, armoured trucks, and tanks begin to roll past. Since our bunker was quite close to the road, soil fell down on us from the constant movement and the bombing, which was quite some distance away.

One night we were completely covered by earth. We could not light our oil knot for fear that the light would shine through, so we had to try to push the soil towards the side of the hole in darkness. We prayed that no more would fall before Krawczuk could support the top of the bunker. I cried when I realized that a large amount of soil might cave in again at any moment and we would be buried alive and suffocate to death. I asked why, after suffering so much and finally having hope that the war — and our misery — would soon end, such a thing had to happen. Four-year-old Eva spoke up, "Mummy, it's better that way. No blood would pour out of us and we would be dead. The Germans are still here. If they shoot us, our blood will pour out."

When Krawczuk finally returned he said that it had been very dangerous to come to our bunker because German soldiers were all over the grounds — in the house, yard, barn, and attics. They were half-frozen and in search of whatever shelter they could find. When he realized what had happened to us, he put his wife on the lookout and brought over small logs, one at a time, and some boards from the shack. We hastily made a support for the top of the bunker while Eva watched from the potato hole. Krawczuk brought us some food and we crawled into the bunker as he replaced the stones in the opening of the potato hole. We returned to darkness: we could still not use our oil knot in case a soldier came into the potato cellar.

For the same reason, we could not even whisper. Eva did not even know how to talk anymore — only to whisper — but now she and Philip were not even permitted to do that. It is difficult to imagine four- and ten-year-old children keeping quiet for days at a time, and how hard it was for us to have to put our hands over their mouths each time they tried to speak. We lost all track of time. We did not know how long it had been since we had last seen Krawczuk. Our food supply was very low and most of what we had we gave to the children. Finally, Krawczuk returned one morning and removed the stones from the opening of the wall. He told us that the Germans were gone and Soviets had been seen in the village. Just before he arrived I had fallen asleep and dreamed that my mother, pointing to masses of beggars and cripples, had said to me, "The Russians are here, do you see those people? Whatever you still own, give it to them, give, give, give." When I awoke I told everyone my dream and Baruch stated, "From your mouth to God's ears."

Instead of feeling relief and happiness about the news, a single thought obsessed me: if it was true that the Germans were gone, then we would probably live. Why should we survive while the rest of our family died such terrible deaths?

We debated what to do next. Baruch announced

that he could not spend a single day longer in the bunker and that the next day at dawn he, Rachel, and Philip were leaving for town. We hesitated to do this since the town was quite far away. Philip was old enough to walk but we would have to carry Eva most of the way and did not feel strong enough. We therefore asked Krawczuk to let Kukurudza know we would like to see him. We wanted to ask him to take us all to town, by horse and buggy, the next morning. But Kukurudza refused, claiming it was dangerous to travel in the dark because the retreating Germans had mined the road in many places and had left explosives even in the fields. He told us that a boy playing near his home had picked up an object and been killed just that afternoon. He also heard that before retreating, the Germans had organized Ukrainian partisans to fight the Soviets and had left them many weapons and ammunition. The partisans were mostly criminals and known murderers. They would hide in the woods during the day but at night they were a danger to anyone they encountered. Kukurudza also refused to take us into town during the day because he was known in all the villages and people might think he had been hiding us.

Despite all this, Baruch and Rachel decided to leave the next morning as planned. Since Leon was better known in the villages than I, we decided that I would walk through the fields to the neighbouring village to ask our friend the priest what he thought we should do. I will never forget that journey. I had not walked for months, because we had been in the bunker, and my muscles had grown weak from inactivity. Since it was spring, the snow had melted and the fields were drenched. Each time I took a step I could hardly pull my legs out of the mud. After a seemingly endless time, I knew I could no longer proceed by foot: I had no other choice but to crawl on my hands and knees the rest of the way. I reached the village covered in mud. Passersby looked at me strangely. Luckily, the church was not too far from the outskirts of the village and I managed to reach it by walking on the sidewalk. When I reached the priest's residence, his mother opened the door. She looked frightened by my appearance and called her son immediately.

The priest recognized me and took me into his study. He asked his mother to see that my coat and boots were cleaned and ordered me a meal. He then advised us not to leave the bunker yet. He had heard on the radio that an entire German contingent had been circled by the strong Soviet army and had no other choice but to retreat through the front near us. It was difficult to say how long this would take or how long they would remain in our village once they had broken through. In the meanwhile, we were safest in the bunker.

The priest sent for his horses and driver to take me back to the bunker. I would not have made it otherwise. We agreed that the driver would let me out where the fields ended and the orchards began so that he would not know exactly where I was going. He also handed the driver a parcel for me. When we reached the designated spot, I watched the driver turn back on the road and walked slowly through a garden until he disappeared. Then I turned in the direction of our bunker. It had begun to get dark. Leon was very worried and had sent the landlady to look for me. When she saw me, she gave me an all-clear signal and I crawled back into the bunker. Leon and Eva were overjoyed to see me.

Leon and I decided to follow the priest's advice and remain in the bunker. The parcel that he had given us contained a loaf of white bread, which we had not had in a long time and kept mostly for Eva, some eggs that our landlady cooked for us, and cookies. We waited for days for the retreat to begin. All was quiet in the villages. The Soviets had gathered in Mielnica. One day there was a lot of movement of Soviets through our village and Krawczuk thought that the Germans would soon follow. To be on the safe side, he gave us some food and replaced the stones in the wall of the potato cellar to seal up the entrance of the bunker. We could not hear a sound from outside.

We again lost all track of time as we sat in complete darkness. Several days must have passed and the waiting seemed endless. We ran out of food except for a bit of sugar in a jar, but we were so desperate we did not feel the need for food or anything else.

When Eva whispered she was hungry we gave her a bit of sugar on our fingertips. We knew we could not go on much longer. We wondered if the Russians or Germans had evacuated the entire village. We had heard of such incidents before. We were afraid that if it had been the Germans, it would mean certain death for us if we came out. Then again, if it had been the Russians, they might consider us German spies and shoot us, too. Our desperation had no limits. Finally, Krawczuk returned with food. He took a single stone out of the entrance to the bunker and asked us if we were still alive. He couldn't believe we could be after going so long without food. He told us to remain quiet, and that he hoped to be able to tell us what was going on soon. Just before he came Eva had whispered that she was tired and wanted to sleep. This was unusual for her but it turned out to be a blessing. Before Krawczuk could put the stone back into place, we heard a loud German voice say, "What do you have there?" Krawczuk blocked the hole with his back and said, "Potatoes, potatoes." The German left.

At that moment I experienced a feeling I have never had before or since. My heart seemed to stop for a moment and I felt a hot stream in the left side of my chest. I am convinced that if Eva had not been fast asleep she would have yelled out in fear when she heard the horrible voice of the German soldier. We all would have been lost, including Krawczuk. Krawczuk hastily replaced the stone. Without a word he left the potato hole, closing the little door behind him.

We again remained in darkness, in a state of severe tension, but at least we knew now that it could not last too long once the Germans had broken through the front. It was also a bit easier to endure since we had some food for Eva. Our gums were sore from not eating for several days and we could eat very little ourselves. We could also hardly sleep. Finally, Krawczuk came and removed all the stones from the entrance to the bunker. He brought us some soup, which we had not had for some time, and told us that the Germans were definitely gone and the Soviets had taken over. Not long after he had sealed up our bunker, the Russians had begun proceeding toward town with the Germans right behind them, shooting. At the same time a heavy snowstorm had started and completely covered the little doors to the potato cellar and chicken coop. That was the reason for the utter silence we had experienced. Krawczuk had not been able to come to us for four days because the Germans were all over the place looking for shelter, and if the deep snow had not covered up the doors they would surely have discovered us. He was glad that the path leading to us had also been covered with snow like the rest of the yard. He said that the Germans had been very cruel to them and had pushed him and his wife and children into the cold pantry while they took over the heated house.

We ate the soup eagerly since we had not been able

to eat much solid food. We were exhausted from tension and lack of sleep. Leon said that all he wanted was to rest; he was unable to even think about what to do next. He took off his clothes, covered himself with his coat, and was soon fast asleep in the bunker. Eva and I were itchy again since we had not been able to delouse for several days, so I sat on the floor of the potato cellar near the crack of the door and tried to remove our lice.

It was then that I heard the rustling. As I listened closely to the growing noise, I became more and more concerned. At first I thought it might be from some abandoned explosives that were activated. I woke Leon and urged him to come out of the bunker. At first he refused; he was still half asleep and could not hear anything. The noise became a roar. While Leon was finally crawling out of the bunker into the potato cellar the entire top of the bunker, including the logs and boards that supported it, caved in with a tremendous crash. We grabbed our coats and the rest of our clothing and ran out of the potato cellar, since we were afraid the same thing would happen there. The ground outside was very muddy from the melting snow and a steady stream of water poured into the bunker. The collapse probably took place not only because of that but also because of the constant movement of the heavy machinery from the German retreat on the nearby road.

Leon hid behind a tree with Eva while I approached the farm house and looked carefully into a window. I saw the landlady alone in a room and I knocked softly. She looked scared when she saw me and came running out. After hearing what had happened she went to get her husband and they led us into their pantry. It was still too cold to stay there, however, so in the evening they called Kukurudza to bring us to his place. There we stayed in an unheated room, but at least we had a bed and blankets and were more comfortable. We asked to find out the condition of the roads and the situation in Mielnica since we wanted to go there as soon as possible. He told us that the road to town seemed safe from explosives because the Soviets used it to travel between Russia proper and the town. He also heard that some Jews were in town, but that others who had hidden in the woods and rushed out towards the first Soviet patrol had been shot, since the Russians did not know which side they were on. Kukurudza said that there were rumours that many partisans had joined the White Russians hiding in the woods and were preparing to fight the Soviets. We were concerned about the rumours and decided we would be safer in Mielnica. We were right.

We asked Kukurudza to dig up whatever possessions we had left and to ask our previous landlady to prepare the things we had left with her. Our belongings were very important to us, for as long as we had something to trade we had hopes of staying alive. We wanted to take everything with us because if it was true that the partisans were preparing to fight the Soviets, we had no way of knowing if we could return to the village.

We had left with the landlady a bed, a crib, a table and chairs, and some kitchenware, all of which we now hoped to be able to use. Kukurudza loaded our things and we started for town at dawn. We arrived in Mielnica early the next morning. We stopped first at Rachel and Baruch's house, which was located in the centre of town, to see if anyone was there. We had no idea where they had been during the German retreat or where they were now. We were pleased and relieved to find them at home. They told us that a short time after they arrived in town, the Soviets had hastily retreated with the Germans on their heels. The snowstorm had already started and they had managed to escape to a burned-out ruin not far away. They hid in the rubble and covered themselves with boards and whatever else they could find. German soldiers who were also looking for shelter from the snow were all around them in the same ruin. My sister and her family could hear them talking. They survived the next few days, shivering from fear, cold and hunger, until the Germans left. The three of them finally returned to their house where a Ukrainian man had been staying while they were away. He left and they took it over.

We unloaded our belongings and moved in with Rachel and her family. Only one percent of the Jewish population of Mielnica had survived: 24 people out of a total of 2,500. We heard that three young

Jewish men whom we had known had appeared the minute the Germans left, but vanished a short time later. Reportedly, one of the young men, a physician, had left a fortune with a Pole and when he came to reclaim it, the Pole killed him. Another young man had gone to his parents' house, which was being occupied by Poles, and then disappeared. The third had gone to a nearby village where his parents had left their belongings; he also never returned.

All the survivors, including ourselves, were in terrible condition, emaciated and barely able to walk. One of Rachel's neighbours who was also a survivor came over and could not even recognize me. I was only 32 years old but I had changed and aged so much that he did not believe it was me even after being told. Eva had developed a severe case of rickets in the bunker and her legs were bent and her abdomen distended. She was very pale and obviously anaemic, but we could not do much for her. There were no facilities for conducting a blood test, no treatments available, and no food for a proper diet. We did not even know anyone in town to contact to trade our things for food, and we were hungry most of the time. Though we were not living in constant fear, as before, we were still uneasy and did not know what to expect.

Gradually, after a few weeks, word spread that there were doctors in town, and people began to call on us for medical attention. Despite the scarcity of food, which affected even the farmers, we were given a little something for the visits. This helped a great deal. Our luckiest break came when Leon was called to treat a sick boy. After examining the child, he prescribed some medication from a pharmacy that had just started functioning again. As payment, the boy's mother offered Leon a box of sulpha that had been left in her house by a Russian who had spent the night there. There was a lot of gonorrhoea among the Russian soldiers, and shortly afterwards a corporal offered Leon 1,000 rubles for enough sulpha to treat his disease.

The Soviets quickly organized themselves in Mielnica. They asked Leon to establish a general hospital that would serve more than 20 villages as well as the military. No other physicians in the entire region had survived. Nonetheless, our salaries were so meagre that Leon planned on seeing patients at home as well. I realized that we could not continue staying with Rachel and Baruch under those conditions, and asked the Soviet officials to find a place for us to live. They found us an apartment on the outskirts of Mielnica, which was not as safe as the centre of town but still satisfactory considering that most of the Jewish homes had been burned out or were without windows, doors, or even floors — all of which had been removed by Ukrainians and Poles as soon as the Jews went into the ghetto. In addition, there was a great scarcity of homes because the Soviets and their families had taken most of the best ones in the centre of town for themselves. They wanted to be near one another for safety reasons, as well; rumours about partisan attacks on the town were growing.

We moved into the house that was assigned to us. We were glad to be in our own place again and to live in peace and quiet, though the pain from the loss of our loved ones stayed with us. After years of being without soap and hot water, we were finally able to clean ourselves up; it felt wonderful. With the little furniture we had, and with some crates covered with sacks filled with straw, we made an examining room. Many patients preferred to come to us rather than to the clinic at the hospital. We couldn't complain: we were allowed to buy things in the only store that existed at the time, which was restricted to party members. It didn't have much, but still people envied us. I bought poor quality stockings for Eva, socks for Leon, and some pieces of material to make dresses.

While we were in hiding, we had a book of children's poems that we would read to Eva in a whisper. She surprised us after a short time by reciting the entire book of poems without missing a single word. She then became interested in the letters of the alphabet and by the time we came out of the bunker, when she was four, she knew them all. In the bunker, her cousin Philip would read in a whisper or write to pass the time, and in no time at all she had learned to read and write from him. She quickly became as fluent in reading and writing in

Polish as any adult, and Philip could not keep up with her. Her favourite pastime was learning to spell. When the bunker collapsed and we had to stay with Kukurudza for a few days, she found a book printed in Gothic letters, left behind by the Germans, and was absolutely intrigued. When we told her what the letters were, she was almost immediately able to read the pages fluently.

In Mielnica people admired Eva and would come over just to hear her read. She was considered a wonderchild. The only problem was that she would frequently read and talk in a whisper, and we would have to remind her to speak in a normal voice. Shortly after the Soviets arrived, they brought over Russian teachers and formed a school and a nursery. We sent Eva to the nursery school. The teacher would read stories to the children in Russian, and Eva would sit close to her, intently watching every word in the book until she could read Russian fluently as well. The teacher reported this to the director of the school board, who asked us if we were aware that our daughter was a genius. They thought she should enter third grade, but since she was not even five years old, we insisted she remain in kindergarten. The school board director ended the conversation we had with him by stating "such children do not live too long." Even if it had been true, one does not have to tell it to the parents, but such is the Russian mentality. On Stalin's birthday there was a big celebration where Eva was selected to open the festivities by reciting a long Russian poem. Such peaceful occurrences did not last long, for there were still many troubles ahead.

10

WHEN THE SOVIETS began to mobilize the local men, it was Leon's job to examine them and determine their level of fitness. (Leon himself had a special document from the first secretary of the party releasing him from military service because he was director of the hospital for the entire area.) It soon became known that those men with very little or no training were sent to the front line (Kanonenfutter) to protect the Soviet soldiers, and were almost all killed during the first attack. All those over age 18, therefore, tried to avoid being enlisted. They would come to our house at night from near and distant villages to offer Leon money and expensive gifts — most likely taken from Jews — to declare them unfit. We would argue and chase them away, but they kept coming back. Some came by horse and buggy and would spend the night in our yard. The minute Leon left the house in the morning, there they were, pleading and begging. We were terrified; if even the slightest suspicion arose that Leon was accepting bribes to declare men unfit, it meant Siberia for him. For some time we continued to answer the door whenever there was a knock, since it might be the hospital or Soviet officials. After a while we agreed that they would have to use a certain kind of knock for us to answer.

Many men — including Baruch — went into hiding to avoid being enlisted. Leon had been afraid to do anything to help our brother-in-law, but a chance finally presented itself. One of the most influential majors at the enlisting commission had gotten a married woman pregnant. He was also married with a family and was anxious for the woman to have an abortion. The nearest gynaecologist who could do the procedure was in Borszczów, so Leon agreed to go to Borszczów to try to find him if Baruch would be released from active service. Since there was no transportation, Leon went by foot. It was a tremendous distance. Rachel accompanied him because she was very anxious that the arrangements for the abortion — and her husband's release from service — were made. On the way they passed a wooded area filled with corpses from a recent battle between partisans and Soviets. They then lost their way and ended up in a little town called Skala, where Leon was interrogated by the Soviet police and released only after the major had been phoned. Finally, they reached Borszczów where the gynaecologist agreed to perform the abortion. When they returned home, the major kept his word and released Baruch from active service, but made him join the local militia instead.

Leon worked constantly. During the day he was either at the hospital, seeing patients at home, or making house calls. From time to time he would work at the enlisting commission, as well. At night he handled emergencies and routine examinations of prisoners. A certificate was required for each one stating that they were fit to make the trip to Siberia. The prisoners were mostly bourgeois. It was a very unpleasant job, but the worst was yet to come.

Whenever the Soviets left town to return to Russia proper, they were attacked by partisans and White Russians and there were many casualties on both sides. After some time the Soviets controlled the towns while the partisans had the villages. The Soviets organized themselves to fight, demanding that Leon accompany them in case they were hurt. When he refused, they threatened to take him to court, saying, "Why is your life more important than ours? We are obligated to fight and so are you." Leon replied that he had already faced death many times and now wanted to live. His refusal to accompany them was a serious matter that could result in his exile to Siberia. The Soviets also engaged the militia to help them in fighting. On one such occasion, Baruch was almost severely injured when a bullet ripped through his heavy fur coat.

On top of this, there were rumours that there were many wounded partisans in the woods who wanted to kidnap us to force us to attend to them. To avoid being caught, we began spending the night with different people whom we knew and trusted. Yet we were never sure what would happen. One winter night there was a bad snowstorm and we decided to sleep at home. We heard a knock on the door and then on the windows. We were unsure if it was the "hospital knock," so we didn't answer and crouched down behind a wall in case of shooting. The knocking continued for some time. When it finally stopped, we looked around the house carefully to make sure that no one was hiding. We then decided that I should go to the hospital because if everything was all right there, it could only have been the Soviet officials wanting to take Leon on a transport to Siberia or the partisans trying to kidnap him. I went to the hospital in the middle of the night in the blinding snowstorm. I found out that drunken Russian soldiers had been in a fight with firearms and one of them had been wounded. A nurse told me that she had sent the doorman to get one of us but since he had been unable to reach us she had checked the soldier herself and stopped his bleeding.

After examining the soldier myself, I went home. It had been very slippery the previous day and the snow had covered the sidewalks so I walked very carefully. Nevertheless, I slipped and fell hard. My back hurt so much that I could barely lift myself up. I managed to get home slowly, but I was in tremendous pain for weeks. Since x-rays were unavailable, all Leon could do for me was to support my back with some straps.

We began to feel desperate, constantly looking for excuses for Leon not to accompany the Soviets on their fights with the partisans. We became particularly concerned when we heard that a Jewish man of about 16, who had survived the Holocaust by hiding in the woods with his mother, was enlisted into the militia. Shortly after being taken to fight the partisans, he was shot to death. The Soviets gave him an honorary funeral that the whole town attended. I will never forget the look on his mother's face as she sat near his coffin and held on to her son.

Rumours began circulating that there had been an agreement between the Russian government and the government of so-called "Poland proper": all Poles had the right to go to Poland proper, and Ukrainians were allowed to remain in the part of Poland that had been annexed by Russia. Jews who had family in Poland proper could go there as well. There were also rumours that in the distant city of Czortkow they were already registering people to go to Poland proper. Since we were so desperate to get out of our situation, we decided that I would go to Czortkow to see if the rumours were true. If we could register there, we would be able to tell the Soviet officials that we were going to Poland proper, and they would have to leave us alone.

It was difficult to get to Czortkow, which was quite far away, since there was no transportation at all.

However, we were friendly with a Russian major who often invited us to his home for dinner. He knew about my back pain, so I told him that I wanted to go to Czortkow to have an x-ray of my spine. The major said that he had heard of a freight wagon leaving soon for Czortkow with members of the party. He supposed that he and other officials would be asked to accompany them, and promised to let me know when they were leaving. However, I would still need permission to travel from the first secretary himself. This I received, but the first secretary did not ask me how I would get there nor did he mention anything about the freight wagon.

One Friday morning, however, the major informed me that the freight wagon would be leaving at noon. He told me to meet him at the train station where he would ask the first secretary to include me in the group. He believed that when the first secretary saw me there he would not refuse me. I prepared myself for the trip. We paid a neighbour to take care of Eva, since Leon worked day and night, and Rachel refused to take her. My sister struggled to have enough food for her own family and was afraid that I might be gone for many weeks — or not return at all.

Leon walked with me to the train station. We hoped that I would be leaving at noon, as the major had said, but we had no idea when I would return. Once we were at the station, the group of officials arrived in a truck. When the first secretary came out, the major convinced him to permit me to come along. Leon left hastily because he had to get back to work, but before the train could start to move, the partisans began shooting at us from all sides. We could hear bullets hitting the wagon as we lay flat on the floor. The partisans could be seen approaching from the distance. I was very frightened; I thought that this was the end of me and I wondered what would become of Eva. Suddenly the train started moving and soon sped away. Leon had heard the shots and ran towards town, where he found out that the train had managed to get through before the partisans had reached the station.

It was already dark when we arrived in Czortkow, so we all spent the night in the wagon. I kept asking when we would be returning, but no one seemed to know. Finally the major told me that they had a lot of business to attend to but they hoped to be able to leave sometime during the following night because they wanted to travel in the dark. He advised me to be at the station and said he would look for me. I worried about having to wait, probably alone, in the dark station lit only by a single kerosene lamp, but I knew I didn't want to miss my ride back.

We walked from the station into the city. A lawyer had been recommended to me for help, but since there were no telephones I had to go to his office and hope that he would see me. After a long wait, he received me. He confirmed the fact that registration would soon start in Czortkow, but said he was sure there was no way we could be registered there. He thought, however, that registration would soon start in Mielnica. I left his office.

It was a warm winter day and the snow was melting, producing floods of water throughout the city. My boots were poor and my feet were completely wet but I had no choice but to walk back to the station. It had taken me so long to reach the lawyer that I didn't think I had enough time to go to the hospital for the x-ray of my spine, especially without an appointment. I went straight to the station and waited, shivering as evening approached and the temperature dropped. I tried to remove my boots to dry my feet a bit, but the boots were swollen from wetness and stuck to my feet. I waited until after midnight until I heard the voices of the major and the rest of the company. We boarded the wagon and it started moving. I was uneasy after the journey there and the tasteless jokes of the company all night annoyed me very much, but I kept quiet and pretended I was asleep. It was still dark when we arrived at the station. A truck waiting for the company brought me to town and dropped me off not far from our place. When I knocked on the bedroom window, Leon was clearly relieved to see me home safely. With great difficulty he helped me off with my boots and into the warm bed. My feet felt like ice.

11

SPRING CAME after my return from Czortkow and with it the good news that registration to Poland proper would soon start. Although we did not know what awaited us in Poland, we knew that we had to get out of the dangerous situation in which Leon could be forced to fight against the partisans at any moment. In addition, we clearly didn't want Eva to grow up where we were. Our mood improved as we started to prepare ourselves for the move. Most important was to get enough food to last a few months, much of which would have to be specially prepared so that it would not spoil. We knew that the first few months in any place during that time were difficult; we therefore had to see that we did not starve.

Finally, the registration began. The minute we put our names on the list, the first secretary of the party called me to his office and expressed his surprise that we wanted to leave. He kept me for over an hour, giving me all sorts of arguments as to why we should remain in Russia. I kept explaining to him that we wished to continue our training in psychiatry in Poland and that we missed our relatives in Przemyśl. We had decided that our chances of advancing in our field would be better there than in a small town like Mielnica. At this, he promised to send us to Moscow for training as soon as things became more stable. I told him again that we appreciated what had been done for us, but we wanted to be with our relatives. (This was untrue, of course, since not a single relative of ours had survived the Holocaust. My father-in-law was killed at the beginning of the war. My mother-in-law went to the gas chambers in Auschwitz, and my sister-in-law died of typhoid fever in the same camp at age 24. My brother-in-law and his wife also perished in Auschwitz. Leon's grandmother had died of starvation and difficult conditions a few months before the rest of the family were taken to Auschwitz.)

I finally decided to get up because I didn't know what else to tell him. He came over to my side of the desk and, putting his hands on both sides of me to prevent me from leaving, said, "I won't let you go until you promise you are staying with us." I insisted again that we were longing to be with our family. He took his arms away and said, "Remember, you were hiding before and you will be hiding again." With this he let me go.

We were uneasy the following weeks, worried that he might find some way to prevent us from leaving. However, spring and early summer passed peacefully and we looked forward to the day when we would be allowed to board the train. In the middle of the summer, there was an announcement that there would be enough space on the train for all registered people and their belongings. We secured a horse and buggy and loaded our provisions: two large sacks of flour; a ten-kilogram sack of homemade dry noodles, buckwheat, sugar, beans, peas, and dried salami; a few pieces of furniture; and some personal and household belongings. There were hundreds of people waiting to board. We were assigned a space on the grass to unload our things and were told to wait for the train.

We waited for almost four full days in the scorching sun and pouring rain. The nights were chilly and we were afraid the partisans would get us. We carried water from the nearby train station and made fires from dry branches, leaves, and whatever else we could find to make a cup of tea. We witnessed scenes between Polish husbands who had decided to go to Poland proper and their Ukrainian wives who wanted to stay behind with their families, or vice versa, and quarrels about their children.

Finally the train — consisting of freight wagons — arrived, and we loaded our belongings and boarded. We were glad to finally be on our way. However, many people had gotten sick over the past few days, and Leon was constantly called to attend to them. When he did not return after a stop, our five-year-old Eva, who was always worried about him, said, "Women have husbands who are with them all the time and they don't have to worry, but we have a husband who is always called away and we worry about him."

We seemed to travel endlessly before stopping in Przemyśl. We never knew how long we would be at a station, but Leon decided to take a chance and run to his parents' house not too far away. I stayed in the wagon with Eva and our belongings. Leon returned soon with bad news: two friends of his, a Jewish lawyer and doctor, had been shot to death by Poles. A man who was staying at his parents' house warned Leon to continue with the transport because it would be too dangerous to stay in chaotic Przemyśl. The train began moving again and our trip continued. Rachel, Baruch and Philip left the train when we reached Katowice in Silesia. We had not been travelling in the same wagon and were therefore taken by surprise when they came to say good-bye. We asked them why they were getting off in Katowice, when the entire transport was continuing further into Silesia, and they replied that they were just tired of travelling.

We continued to the next stop in Bytom where we soon discovered that we also should have stayed in Katowice, since the only large Jewish centre and a Jewish Congress had been formed there. Leon and another Jewish man looked for a way for us to make the short trip back to Katowice. Meanwhile, Eva was bitten by an insect and her ear became very swollen. She soon developed a fever, but there was nothing we could do for her except put moist compresses on her ear and give her aspirin.

Leon soon found a conductor who was willing to take us back to Katowice in exchange for some of our provisions. The Jewish man who had been on the earlier train with us was well-informed about conditions in Katowice and told us that there would be some representatives from the Jewish Congress who would help us. There were, and they provided us with transportation to large wooden barracks abandoned by the German military. In one small building they gathered Jews, in another, Poles, and in distant buildings a large number of Russian soldiers wearing Polish uniforms. They exercised to Polish commands, but could be heard speaking in Russian among themselves.

We were given a tiny, low-ceilinged room that could hold a single bed in which the three of us slept, and a small table with three chairs. There was an iron stove, but we couldn't get any wood or coal to make warm food in it. I went around the camp and gathered enough dried branches to boil water for tea.

For several weeks, we stayed in this small room in the wooden barracks. On sunny days it was mercilessly hot, on rainy nights very cold. When fall approached, we went daily to the city to try to find warmer accommodations for the winter and to look for a way to make some money, since our supplies were very low.

We got a lock and key to close up the room each time we left, but one evening, on our way home, people in our building told us that teenage Polish boys had broken into our room and had taken whatever they wanted. When we got to our room, there was nothing left but the bed.

A rage came over me and, almost without thinking, I ran straight to the building where the Poles lived, with Leon, Eva and a young neighbour from our building running after me. The neighbour said he could recognize the boys who had broken in, so we went from room to room until he recognized one. I angrily demanded that our belongings be returned. The boy said that he had only taken my daughter's bed, which was standing packed away since we had no place for it. We soon retrieved the bed and our neighbour took it back to our room. The boy then told us that most of our other things were taken by a professor's children. We burst into the professor's room and saw our chairs. Other people in the building entered the room and tried to prevent us from searching. We pushed them away and quickly spotted some of our clothes and bedding. Our neighbour returned to make another trip to take our things back to our room. A crowd soon gathered in the professor's room and told him not to let us search any further. We were sure they were ready to harm us. When our neighbour returned from his next trip, he begged us in Yiddish to leave, warning us that our lives were in danger. I left with great hesitation, thinking how hard it had been to gather and prepare our provisions that would now be used by those murderers.

Leon went to the Jewish Congress the next day to complain, while I remained in our room with Eva; we could not even close our door and had to keep a chair in front of it. The Congress did not have time to do anything about our problem, and advised us instead to search for a place in the city so we could leave the barracks as soon as possible. For the next few days one of us would go into the city to look for housing, while the other remained in the room.

Finally, Leon met a man through my brother-in-law who knew of a room vacated by a German woman who escaped from Katowice. Her relative lived in most of the apartment, but the man said she would agree to rent us a vacant room if we gave her some money up front. We sold Eva's only leggings and top and a warm coat and gave the money to the man. He took us to the place and the woman gave us the key to our room, which was full of furniture and had no place for ours. At the man's suggestion we put our things in the attic, but it was accessible to everyone in the three-storey house, and we weren't happy about it.

A few days later, the woman decided that she would keep our things for us in her part of the apartment. When we went up to the attic, however, there was no sign of them. What's more, we then found out that the woman had never asked nor received any money for the room. She reproached the man in our presence but he only walked away without a word. We did not sleep for nights because there were bedbugs and cockroaches, but we knew we couldn't afford anything else. We cleaned the bed as much as we could, but it was never free of bugs. We spent more than a year under those conditions.

It was impossible to earn a living as a doctor. We were afraid to even admit we were physicians since several Jewish doctors had been murdered in their Katowice offices by the Polish underground, the "A.K." It had happened at the same time one afternoon. A man went to each of their offices and told the receptionists that they had no appointment but were willing to wait until the other patients were seen. They then went in and shot the doctors. I therefore travelled deep into Silesia using a Polish name, bought whatever clothes I could and then sold them in Katowice, where there was a great scarcity of everything. Leon could not do this because he looked Jewish and whenever he tried to help me he was caught by the Polish police. It was always difficult to get him out of the police station and whatever he had with him was always confiscated. Life was difficult when I went on those trips. I worried about Eva and Leon and they worried about me, and about my suspicious I.D. card that could get me into trouble.

12

A NUMBER OF UNPLEASANT INCIDENTS occurred during our stay in Katowice. One day there was a great commotion in the house where we lived because the Polish police were searching each of the apartments. They came to our room and without saying a word messed up every shelf and drawer and threw things on the floor. Finally they got hold of a small bottle of alcohol that Leon had received from a patient before we arrived that was our only means of sterilizing skin before an injection or cleaning wounds. The police sniffed the alcohol and accused us of producing moonshine. We explained that this was ridiculous — how could we have produced it — but they didn't believe us. They then found a few decagrams of yeast that I had bought to bake bread and insisted that this was further proof of our producing alcohol.

They took us to a remote police station. Eva had to come with us because we didn't have time to leave her with friends. They took Leon in for questioning while she and I waited for hours outside the room. It was almost dark by the time a policeman finally came out and told us we could go home — without Leon. When I asked him why my husband could not come with us he said he was unable to say.

Instead of going home, I went straight to some of our cousins to tell them what had happened. They lived in a very nice building — though also in one room — filled with furniture and beautiful household goods left behind by Germans who were collaborating with the Gestapo and had run away to Germany. My cousins knew a party member in the Polish government who might be able to help us. He was not at home, but his wife promised that he would intervene on Leon's behalf as soon as he could. Apparently, he came home very late that night and inquired about Leon the next morning. As a result, the police told Leon that they were sending the alcohol for chemical analysis and depending on the outcome, they would know how to deal with him. Meanwhile, they let him go. They probably drank the alcohol the minute he left the office. We never heard from them again, but the sleepless night that Leon and I had gone through was not easy to forget.

Another incident occurred that was even more serious. Leon had heard of a lawyer with connections to consulates who managed to get visas for people for a fee. Since we, like many others, wished to get out of anti-Semitic Poland as soon as possible, Leon decided to see him. When he left, I was busy running errands and he did not have a chance to tell me where he was going. Eva and I returned at lunch time and were surprised to find him gone. We waited a bit and then went to the post office where I was sure he was waiting for an important phone call we were expecting about selling our house in Przemyśl. When the phone call came through and Leon wasn't there, I knew something was wrong. I couldn't make a decision about the house without consulting him, and the party on the other end of the line thought I was trying to stall; they never called again.

I returned home where there was still no sign of Leon. I waited until supper time and then took Eva to my cousins. Leon's uncle, who was living in Katowice at the time and was very devoted to us, was there. We decided first to ask the party member's wife to use their telephone to call all the hospitals in the city in case he had been in an accident. They had no record of him. The party member was away and his wife expected him the next day, Saturday, so Leon's uncle took me and Eva home. On the way we passed the Jewish Congress, where he interrupted the services in a loud, pleading voice and asked if anyone knew where Leon was or what had happened to him. He begged the people there to help us and gave our address so that they could let us know as soon as they heard anything. He stayed with us all night, but there was no news.

I was so restless after our sleepless night that all I could do was pace up and down our small room, waiting for Eva to awaken so that we could go to my cousins. Around noon, the neighbour came to tell us that her husband had found out that Leon was in a jail for political prisoners and was being interrogated. He didn't know why he was there, but he was afraid that Leon might be taken in a transport leaving for Russia — probably Siberia — that day. The neighbour promised to act as quickly as he could and told me to bring a parcel with a shirt or two, underwear, and some food to the jail immediately. He said that if the parcel was accepted, it meant Leon would remain in jail. If, however, it was refused, it might signal that he was already on his way to Russia.

I left Eva with my cousins, went home to prepare the parcel, and hurried by foot to the jail, several miles away on the outskirts of town. On the way I ran into the man who had lied and taken money from us for our room. He had heard what had happened to Leon and told me that he could free him for a tremendous amount of money that would have to be given to him immediately. I gave him an angry look and told him I was in too much of a hurry to talk. As I ran I thought to myself what a terrible world we live in: I was in a horrible state and the man wanted more money from me than I could scrape together if I sold the last shirt off my back and borrowed from relatives and friends. What's more, I knew he couldn't have helped us anyway.

When I arrived at the jail, there were hundreds of people waiting to hand in their parcels. I took my place in line. After the sleepless night and almost 24 hours without food, I was faint and exhausted. At times I was convinced that I would not be able to continue standing in the scorching sun. Somehow I managed to reach the little window where an official searched the parcel and then took it. He then directed me to wait in another line where I would find out if it was accepted. The sun was no longer as hot when I took my place in the second line. When I reached the little window again it had started to get dark. The parcel was returned to me. I was convinced that Leon was on his way to Siberia. Crying, I went straight to my cousins' where again the neighbours promised to find out what had happened the next morning. I was utterly exhausted and decided to go home for the night to be with Eva.

Once home I lay down with Eva on our bed and fell asleep without even undressing. A knock on the door woke me. It was Leon. He was even more exhausted than I, but he told me what had happened. On the Friday morning that I had gone with Eva to sell used clothes to buy food for the weekend, he had decided to go see the lawyer about exit visas to neighbouring countries, especially Austria. The minute he entered the lawyer's office, two policemen arrested him. When he told them that he had come to see the lawyer, they said that he was not there, but that Leon would have a chance to explain why he wanted to see him at the police station. There were a few others in the lawyer's office who had probably been told the same thing. They were all told that they would be accompanied to the station by two policemen. On the way they were not to look to the right, left, in front, or behind, but only down. They would be shot if anyone approached them.

Since they were not far from where we lived, Leon was petrified that someone might see him and greet him. Yet they finally arrived at the police station and he was led into a cell. He was alone all day, without food. Later, almost as soon as he had fallen asleep, he was woken and taken for interrogation. He told them only the truth, but the questions were twisted in such a way as to try to get him to make a mistake. The same procedure was repeated later that night and again in the morning. Each time the guard saw that Leon had fallen asleep, he would wake him and take him for interrogation. In the morning he was given some food, then released. I am sure that the intervention of my cousin's neighbour helped him; otherwise, he might have been mistreated in jail indefinitely.

After that incident, it became even clearer to us that we had to get out of Poland before Leon perished. He led a very inactive life at the time. He could not work as a physician because Jewish doctors had been shot to death in their offices by the Poles. He could not earn a living doing anything else for the same reason: he clearly looked Jewish. He spent most of his time looking after Eva while I bought and sold secondhand things to make money. We barely made ends meet.

13

SOME FRIENDS from Leon's hometown lived in Warsaw at that time and came to Katowice frequently to buy used clothes to resell in Warsaw at higher prices. They often came to us for meals and to store their merchandise since we lived near the centre of town. I expressed a desire to go to Warsaw, not only to earn more money but also to try to obtain a visa from one of the many consulates there. I wanted first to go to the American consulate, since we had applied there for a visa in 1938 and had been informed that we were on a waiting list and that our turn would come in 1941. The reply had miraculously survived the war, so I had something on paper to show them. Leon's friends invited me to stay with them, so I bought two men's coats and other used clothes, packed a suitcase, and left for Warsaw with Eva. I worried about leaving her with Leon in case something happened to him.

The trip to Warsaw will remain fresh in my memory until my dying day. We arrived at the train station early in the morning, but could not find any transportation into the city. We walked for hours — not sure of our direction — before we even saw an intact house. For miles there were only piles of stones and bricks, destroyed houses turned to rubble, and not a soul in sight. Before the war, Warsaw was a city of two million people. I had never known it well, but even if I had I would never have been able to orient myself in all the ruins. There was nothing to guide us but an occasional street sign. I just walked, dragging poor Eva and the suitcase, according to some directions I had received from our friends. I was relieved when we finally came across someone who confirmed that we were headed the right way. Late that afternoon we came across three whole houses in a row and I knew we were in the right spot.

It turned out that our friends had unexpected visitors and our stay would be inconvenient for them, but we were exhausted and had no other place to go. We spent an uncomfortable night on a small couch. In the morning we rose early and went to the American Consulate. There was a long wait. We took our place in line and finally got into an office where I showed an official my written reply and asked for a visa. A young woman took the card from me and brought it to the Consul. She returned after a few minutes and told me that we would have to reapply for a new affidavit; the promise from 1938 was no longer valid. I was very annoyed and demanded to see the Consul. I had come from Katowice under difficult conditions and thought I deserved at least to see him. She again took the card and went back to the Consul. She returned with the same reply and assured me that the Consul could do nothing for us. My hopes were shattered.

I managed to speak to the Bolivian and Chilean Consuls, but received negative replies from them as well. We started back to our friends' but were so tired from walking that we had to stop frequently to rest. It was almost dark when we arrived, and they were waiting for us outside. They told us they were very worried about us because it was not unusual for people to be dragged into the building ruins at night and robbed of their clothing and anything else they might have. If they were lucky, they were then freed, naked but unharmed.

We slept better that night since we were so exhausted. The next morning I put on the two men's coats, gathered the other things in a bundle, and went with Eva to the market to sell them. With some difficulty I sold the smaller things. Late in the afternoon, I sold one of the coats to a man for a reasonable price. He told me he was sure he had someone who would buy the other one and asked if we would go home with him so his friend could see it. For some reason I trusted this man, and because it was too late to return to my friends, I agreed. I was not wrong. When we arrived at his place, his wife and children were there. She offered us something to eat and his friend came over and bought the coat. They let us spend the night on their couch and in the morning I returned to our friends', gathered our belongings, and left for the train station. I felt we couldn't survive another exhausting day in Warsaw. We arrived in Katowice in the morning and went straight to bed. I was sore from carrying the heavy things, but I could not sleep; the disappointment from not getting a visa was great, and Leon and I kept debating what to do next.

A short while after that, Eva got sick with a temperature that lingered for some time, and we decided to consult a paediatrician. He advised us to take her out of Katowice as soon as possible because it was in a coal mining region and had badly polluted air. Before the war, we had worked in a mental hospital in Otwock, one of the nicest resorts near Warsaw. It was in the woods where the air was light and pure. Leon and I decided that Eva and I would go to Warsaw again and from there to Otwock for the remaining two months of the summer. I bought some secondhand clothes to earn money while we were there.

We arrived in Warsaw early in the morning and I sold the things quickly so we could leave for Otwock by noon. When we arrived in Otwock, we could find no transportation. At last a man with a hand wagon appeared and agreed to bring us to a place where rooms with kitchen privileges were rented. We put our luggage and Eva on the wagon and started out. The man ran so fast that I could not keep up with him, and I could hear Eva screaming for me. I begged him to slow down. Almost two hours later, we reached the rented rooms. They were not too bad or expensive, and I was pleased to find that a friendly neighbour from my hometown was staying in the same place. Her husband had lost a leg in the Russian army towards the end of the war and was being treated in a military hospital nearby. She showed me where to buy food. I devoted all my time to Eva and she soon regained her health.

The month passed. We communicated frequently by mail with Leon, who seemed to be managing well alone, but one day my neighbour ran in to tell me that he had just arrived. He had decided to come as soon as he heard that overseas mail had started to circulate from Warsaw. We were eager to write our family in Canada and the United States, and we wanted to arrange to go to more consulates for a visa anywhere outside of Poland. My neighbour agreed to watch Eva and we left early the next morning for Warsaw. The first thing we did was to send registered letters to my brother Willy and Leon's uncle. (We found out later that not until they received them did they know that we were alive and what had happened to the rest of the family.) They immediately telephoned my uncle, who wanted to see the letter. My brother sent it to him under the condition that he send it back. Leon's uncle asked my uncle who lived in New York to come over to read the letter, since he was afraid it would get lost in the mail.

We got our passports on the spot in Warsaw, but once again were unsuccessful at the consulates. We returned to Otwock where Eva was as happy to see us as we were to see her. We remained there for another month, then wrote our cousins in Katowice to ask them to check on our room from time to time until we returned. The two month stay did a lot of good for Eva and for all of us. Yet fall was approaching and we had to return to Katowice to figure out how to survive the winter.

When we returned, I went to the consulates in Katowice, beginning with the Austrian Consulate. I was permitted to see the consul and explained to him that we realized it would take a long time to go to the United States but that if we could leave for a Displaced Persons (D.P.) camp in Austria, it would simplify the process. He gave me the needed transit visa on the spot. This was surprising, since a transit visa is legally issued only to someone who has a visa for a final destination and has to pass through another country on the way. However, I was happy and grateful to him and did not ask any questions. A friend of ours from the university happened to be in Katowice at the time and begged me to try to get a visa for him as well. I waited a few days and then got one for him, too, without difficulty. He returned to Katowice a week later and begged me again to get more visas for his cousin and her son. Again, I had no difficulty getting them. We agreed to leave Poland together soon.

We prepared enough food, flour, sugar, and buckwheat to last two or three months. We had agreed to meet our friends from Warsaw at the train station there, but getting from the Katowice train to the one that went directly from Warsaw to Vienna was difficult because they were far apart and time was limited. Although our friends were there and had reserved a place for us, two of them had to meet us while one reserved our place. It was difficult to drag all our luggage even with their help, and after we boarded the train we realized that an important piece was missing. We could not understand how it had happened. Leon ran in the direction of the Katowice train and found it at the door of the coach before the train started to move. We both worried he wouldn't make it back in time and I stood nervously on the coach steps until I saw him return.

Our visas were not questioned and we passed through the Austrian border without difficulty. We arrived in Vienna in the morning. There was no transportation available, but we found a man with a hand wagon to load our luggage while we walked behind him. Our friends knew of a reasonable hotel that their relatives had reserved for us and we soon settled in. There was no food available; had we not brought our own supplies, we certainly would have starved.

Together with our friends, we decided to begin to work immediately. We had concealed the fact that we were medical doctors in Poland for long enough, and we now asked the Joint Distribution Committee (JDC) to assign us work as camp doctors. We were advised, however, that there was a greater need for such physicians further on in Salzburg, Hofgastein, or Badgastein, so a few weeks later we decided to relocate. From Vienna we had to pass through the Russian section of Austria, where Russian officials stopped us to ask who we were, where we were from, and where we were going. One of our friends replied that we were Greeks on our way home. There were no more questions, and we passed through safely.

When we arrived in Salzburg, we were taken directly to a wooden camp. There were about 40 to 50 people to a large barrack, and we each got a bunk bed. There was a common outdoor toilet for women and another for men. I found this very unpleasant because several people had to use it at the same time, and I became constipated because I just could not use it in the company of others. Luckily, we were not there for long, since fall was approaching and the camp was not heated.

The JDC next transferred us to Camp Riedenburg, which was more centrally located and consisted of brick buildings with small iron stoves in each room. Most of the people stayed in large rooms with as many as 50 people to a room, but as doctors we received a separate small room for ourselves. We were also given three iron beds, two small tables, benches, and a cupboard and iron stove. We made the room as comfortable as we could, covering up our suitcases with table cloths and using them as night tables. We immediately started working at the camp hospital. Leon was in charge of a ward of physically ill inpatients and took care of occasional psychiatric cases. When a mentally ill patient required hospitalization, he was referred to the local mental hospital, since there were no facilities at the camp. I looked after a very busy outpatient department for the physically ill and ran the children's health clinic.

Eva started school in the camp. It was mainly a Hebrew school, but she also learned English. Some of our old friends were in the camp, and with Eva we made new friends as well. After a time we had quite a good social life there, and frequently attended the theatre and opera in Salzburg and took trips to Hofgastein, Badgastein and other beautiful places in the Alps. Meals were provided to us by the camp kitchen, and we were given extra provisions and a small salary for our work.

Leon was soon asked by the JDC to organize a hospital in Hallein, which he did in addition to his work in the camp. A car picked him up early in the morning and took him for a half day into Hallein. In the afternoon, he looked after his ward at the camp hospital. For the first time since the war we felt free and unafraid. Yet we still hoped to start a new life on our own and eagerly wanted to leave the camp as soon as possible.

14

WE HAD BEEN CORRESPONDING with my brother Willy in Canada and our uncles in New York but they were apparently unable to speed up our immigration into either country. However, there were rumours that the JDC would soon register people for a transport leaving for Canada or the United States. We waited in hope. Winter set in and we went about our daily lives. In the spring there was a registration for a transport to Canada for those whose relatives in Canada would pay for the trip. We were not among them. Willy wrote us that he had contacted the Jewish Congress in Montreal and had been promised that they would bring us over. We inquired why we were not on the list and were told that there would soon be another registration for an additional transport and we would probably go then. We were disappointed because that transport did not leave until the end of the summer.

After people began leaving the camp, we were offered a larger room in another building. Soon after we moved, registration started. A few weeks later we had to go through medical examinations and many tests and then we prepared ourselves for the trip. Our suitcases, which had survived the war, were nonetheless shabby, and we did not think they could withstand the long trip. They would surely have fallen apart and we would have lost the few belongings we possessed. We went to the shopping area of Salzburg to look for some luggage but found none. We finally heard of a man who made slip-covers for suitcases from light blankets or strong linens, so we sacrificed our blankets.

The day finally came when we joined a group of people from our camp on a train to the German port of Bremen to wait for the ship. We left the camp at the beginning of January 1948 and had to wait for three weeks in crowded barracks where 15 to 20 people slept in a room. The food was inadequate but we fortunately had the provisions we had prepared. Three weeks later we boarded the S.S. General Sturgess.

The military ship had a capacity of 10,000 tons. Since the actual load consisted only of a few tons and the ocean was very rough in February, the ship was tossed around like a ball. As soon as we started to move we felt seasick. Men and women stayed in separate cabins. Eva and I got upper berths, since it was a small cabin, and the two lower berths were assigned to an elderly woman and a woman with a small baby. During the night, as the ship was wildly thrown about, I vomited constantly and felt so weak I could not even lift my head to see how Eva was doing. She moaned constantly and when things got very rough called out, "I am afraid I will fall!" All I could do was beg her to hold on tightly to an iron bar over the head of her bed, as I was doing. If we hadn't, we surely would have been thrown out of bed and broken our bones. I tried to talk to her constantly, afraid that if she fell asleep she might release the bar and fall out of bed. (Months after arriving at my brother's, Eva would still hold onto the headboard at night.)

For days we could not eat or move. Leon managed somewhat better and came over several times a day to urge us to at least drink some liquids that he brought us, but we could not hold anything in our stomachs. We thought we might be able to keep some fruit down, but we never had any. By chance Leon met the ship doctor, an American, and asked him whether he could trade some American cigarettes he had earned for some fruit. The doctor gladly agreed. Leon traded him a few cartons of cigarettes for two apples and the doctor told him they should meet every day at the same place and he would give him a few more pieces of fruit each time. He never showed up again and Leon was unable to find him during the rest of the trip. We didn't make an issue of it; we enjoyed the two apples and were able to keep them down.

We arrived in Halifax, Nova Scotia on February 11, 1948. After waiting at the port for some time we boarded a train headed for Montreal that was supposed to take us directly to Perth, Ontario, where Willy had lived since 1930. The train stopped in

Montreal and many people got off to meet their relatives. We, however, knew that our final destination was Perth and did not prepare to get off. Suddenly a man came over to us, introduced himself as Willy's brother-in-law, Martin Pedovitch, and told us that my brother was at the train station in Montreal. We were to hurry and get off before the train started moving again. We were suspicious after all we had gone through in the war and couldn't figure out how this man knew who we were and why Willy had not come for us himself. It took the man some time to convince us that he was who he said he was and that the reason Willy had not come on board himself was that he had not been permitted to do so. We took our luggage and left the train.

Willy ran to greet us. Almost in a daze we were taken straight to Pedovitch's home where my aunt, cousins and other relatives whom I did not even know were waiting. There was a big reception for everyone who had come to meet us but it was more than I could handle. I broke down, crying, bitterly repeating, "Why did we survive, why did we deserve to survive, when the rest of our relatives, our parents, sisters, brother, died such terrible deaths?" In my immediate family alone I had lost my parents, a sister and brother-in-law and their teenage son and daughter, another sister and brother-in-law and their eight-year-old son, and my beloved brother in his twenties. We also lost aunts and uncles and their children and grandchildren.

My husband lost his parents, grandmother, brother and sister-in-law, as well as his beloved sister, aunts, uncles and cousins.

After the reception, the family argued over where we would spend the night. Everyone wanted us in their own home. Finally we went to my aunt and cousins' for the night. After breakfast Willy picked us up and took us to meet a few of his friends before leaving for his home in Perth. We drove through freezing rain to Willy's friend's home in Smith Falls where we left the car and continued to Perth by train.

It was supper time when we arrived at his home and met his wife Lily and their two children, Earl and Miriam, for the first time. My aunt and uncle and cousin from New York were also there, and I was glad to see them. They spent a few days with us, and then Leon's uncle from New York came to visit us. I had never met him before, but Leon thought he had changed. He looked much older and had lost his sense of humour and desire to socialize. Later, when we visited New York, his relatives told us that the change in him occurred suddenly when at the beginning of the war he found out that his beloved brother, my father-in-law, had been one of Hitler's first victims in Poland. After that he became depressed, could not eat or sleep, and had to receive treatment.

After resting for a week or so we started to attend night classes in English for immigrants. We did not know a word but after a few weeks realized that the classes weren't helping: most of the students were farmers who could barely read. It took three hours to get through one page. We asked Willy to explain to the teacher how important it was for us to make progress so we could begin to work. We were permitted to attend high school classes for a while after that but they were too advanced. Willy spoke to the teacher again and asked him to give us private lessons once or twice a week, for which we were willing to pay with the little bit of money we had. The teacher agreed, and we learned the basics of the language in a few short weeks.

Eva started school at about the same time. In camp she had led her third grade class, but the first day we brought her to school the principal pointed to a table and door and asked her to name them in English. She could not. She was placed in first grade and was very unhappy. After two weeks, however, she was ahead of her class in arithmetic and other subjects and the teacher moved her to second grade. She still got bad grades in English, however, and each time she received her marks she was so ashamed to come home that she stayed outside crying. Whenever she didn't come home on time, we assumed that's where she was and went out to get her. She blamed us because we had moved so much, while she had wanted to stay in the camp in Salzburg.

As soon as our English improved, Leon went to Montreal to look for work. He discovered that we would have to begin with a year of internship, but that in Quebec one had to be a Canadian citizen to get the Enabling Certificate to take the Dominion Council Examinations. Since that meant a five-year wait, we decided to go to Toronto, instead, where we both got internships but were told not to approach the College of Physicians and Surgeons for certification until our English improved.

We longed to establish ourselves as quickly as possible since we were both in our late thirties by this time and wanted to be on our own. The internships started on 1 July, but we were advised to begin a month early to observe the interns from the previous year. That meant we had two more months to wait at Willy's. We had already been with his family for more than six weeks and worried that it would be too much for our sister-in-law. Willy suggested that since Easter vacation was approaching, we go to New York to see all the relatives we had not yet met. He took us to Ottawa to get permission to go to the States, and we left by car for New York.

We stayed with some cousins there who were happy to have us. One evening they invited a number of relatives over to collect donations for us. We were shocked and forbade them to do it. In less than two months we would be working in Toronto and would manage on what we would earn. We were insulted that they could even think of giving us charity. However, we would have accepted a loan from a relative or two — in fact, it would have helped us a great deal — but no one offered us one. When we approached one cousin he said he could not lend us more than a hundred dollars. We knew he could give more, but accepted the loan since we needed it so badly. When we started working in Toronto, earning $75 each per month, we bought a money order from the first hundred dollars and repaid my cousin.

15

WE COMFORTED OURSELVES with the thought that once we started working, things would be different. We still had two more months until our internship at Mount Sinai Hospital began. We also knew that we would have to leave Eva at Willy's in Perth, where she was in school, since we could not make a home for her on the small salary we were promised and because we were required to stay in the hospital. We tried to learn English and made the best of our remaining months there. We spent two weeks with a cousin in Montreal, which somewhat helped to shorten our stay.

Everything was new and difficult when we arrived at Mount Sinai because we simply did not yet know enough English. The other physicians were very busy and when they told us something about a patient or gave us preoperative or postoperative orders, we usually could not grasp what they said. They also didn't like being asked to repeat themselves. The administrator, however, was a marvellous man. He immediately tried to make us feel comfortable, ordering uniforms and white shoes for us and trying hard to find an English teacher who could tutor us several evenings a week.

Although the hospital had only 120 beds, it had a high turnover and with only four interns the work was very hard. The month of June was tolerable because there were additional interns from the previous year. It became almost unbearable when they left, however, because we were two out of three interns for a while since the hospital couldn't find a fourth. We worked extremely long hours, beginning at eight o'clock in the morning when we scrubbed for operations, continuing through the afternoon when we worked at a busy emergency clinic taking histories and physicals and seeing patients, and into the evening and night, when we worked in the lab and delivered babies. We were also very lonely for Eva. Every few weeks, when we had a weekend off, we would visit her in Perth. In July she had her tonsils removed, and spent a few days with us in our interns' quarters while she recuperated.

The administrator had told us not to approach the College of Physicians until our English improved. After four months of working with patients and studying English, we thought we not only understood the language sufficiently but also communicated well enough to approach the College. To our regret we found out that although they did not require citizenship (as Quebec did) they refused to promise us anything until we successfully completed the year of internship. We decided to inquire about conditions at colleges in other provinces. Saskatchewan was the only one that could assure us an Enabling Certificate after a year of internship, so shortly after that we applied and were accepted at the Grey Nuns' Hospital there. The administrator at Mount Sinai was very understanding when we explained that we had to do what was best for our future.

Leon went first to see the conditions at the Grey Nuns' Hospital and to find a place for Eva to live, since we wanted to move her closer to us. I then went to Perth, packed up our belongings, and went with Eva by train to Regina. Unfortunately, Leon had only been able to find a place for Eva on the other side of town from the hospital. It was with an elderly couple living in a rather shabby house, but she had a room of her own and school was nearby, an important consideration in the bitterly cold climate of Saskatchewan.

The work was easier at the Grey Nuns' Hospital. Although it was a 500-bed hospital, there were about 16 to 18 interns and our hours were not quite as bad. We did a rotating internship, with two months each of surgery, internal medicine, paediatrics, oncology, obstetrics and gynaecology, and urology. When we weren't on call we spent evenings with Eva, and at least one of us tried to be with her every day. Yet there were some peculiar rules at the hospital. Leon, for example, was given a very large room with two big beds, a large cupboard, plenty of chairs, and a desk and table, but I was not allowed to stay with him. I was given a tiny room with minimal furniture in the nurses' quarters. Although we had been told by the Sister Superior that Eva was invited to visit and eat meals with us when we were not on call, we got into a lot of trouble when she was discovered sleeping in the empty bed in Leon's room. Though she was only nine years old, she had to sleep in my room. From then on, she slept at the foot of my small bed. We were both quite uncomfortable and I hardly slept, but the Sister Superior was so upset with us that I did not want to bother her further. She was not the same towards us after that — and then matters got worse.

Since most of the people who took in boarders were usually poor and had little space, Eva's landlady asked me to store her summer things elsewhere during the winter. I hung her little dresses in the nearly empty cupboard in Leon's room. When spring came, one of the sisters was walking around the interns' quarters seeing what needed to be painted when she looked into the cupboard. "Ladies' clothes in a man's cupboard!" she exclaimed, and I was immediately called by the Sister

Superior and severely reprimanded once again. From then on, whenever I greeted her she turned her head away.

During that year we had many difficulties boarding Eva. The elderly woman was able to keep her for only two months before having to leave to care for her sick daughter in the United States. We tried desperately to find another place for her, and were soon contacted by the parents of a classmate and girlfriend of Eva. They agreed to take her in but said she would have to share a room with their daughter. Though they were quite well-off and did not want to accept money, we insisted on giving them the same amount we had paid Eva's first landlady. After about two weeks, they said we would have to find another place for our daughter because our visits disturbed their privacy. We next found her a place with some poor people who also had a daughter, but Eva had to change schools and was bitterly unhappy about it. In addition, the little girl was very spoiled and jealous of her, and made her life miserable. She would not allow Eva to even come near her toys. Luckily, just before it became really unbearable, the parents of another classmate invited her to stay with them and Eva said that she felt at home with them in a way she had never felt in the three Jewish homes. Those people became our friends, and when we left Regina they came to the railroad station and showered Eva with gifts. We corresponded with them for many years.

When the school year was over, we still had two months remaining of our internship, so we accepted Willy's invitation to send Eva to spend the summer at his place with his children. We worried a great deal about Eva making such a long trip by herself: two days and one night on the train. I went as far as Winnipeg with her, then put her on a train to Montreal where she would then change to Perth. I tried to alert the conductor that she was aboard, but his breath reeked so much of alcohol that I doubted he heard anything I said. We worried constantly until a telegram came from Willy saying she had arrived safely.

16

WE STUDIED during every free moment of our internship year, beginning with pathology, which we found very difficult. When we read a page we would stop every few minutes to look up a word and write out its meaning. By the time we finished the page we had no idea what we had read, and had to go over it again and again until we understood both the words and content. Since Eva was with Willy, we devoted every free evening and weekend to study. Our English slowly progressed.

We decided to ultimately find a place to live in Regina when our internship was finished. We would try to borrow some money from the Jewish Congress and commit ourselves exclusively to studying for the Dominion Council Examinations so that we could establish ourselves. We planned to stay in Saskatchewan in the meanwhile since we thought that conditions for newcomers were better there than elsewhere.

It was difficult to find a place to live because most people refused to accept families with children. We finally found a woman attendant from the hospital who lived nearby with two boys ages 10 and 12 who agreed to rent us a flat consisting of two very small attic rooms. We would also have kitchen privileges. We planned to stay there for the winter, so we immediately started working on making the two filthy rooms liveable. The woman gave us an old couch and a table and we bought a folding bed for Eva and a small table with four chairs. The rest we furnished with orange crates, making bookshelves and dressers. I bought some cheap material and made curtains and covers. We tried to make it as homey as we could with the little money we had and by the time Eva returned from Willy's, everything was ready.

Shortly afterwards she started at a local school and we resumed our intensive studying. We finally received our Enabling Certificates and hoped to write the Dominion Council Examinations in Montreal in the spring. Yet, again, things did not turn out as planned. Our new landlady and her sons were very noisy, constantly fighting and screaming in their downstairs apartment. I could hardly prepare a meal or even heat up a drink for Eva without the boys harassing me — deliberately combing their hair near the stove so that the water from their comb splashed into our food and drink. Life there was unbearable. When the cold weather set in, our two attic rooms felt like the outdoors. We could not sleep no matter how well we covered ourselves. Around that time we received word from the Jewish Congress that they would not lend us any money, and that we would have to apply to the Congress in Montreal. We decided to go there in person and stay until it was time for the examinations.

We asked a friend to store our belongings, then wrote to Willy, who had moved to Montreal with his family, to tell them that we were returning. We took Eva out of school. When we arrived in Montreal in the morning, Willy was already at work. My sister-in-law opened the door and appeared very surprised to see us since she had not yet received our letter. We assured her that we would immediately look for a place to live. When Willy came home, he suggested that Eva stay with them so that we would need only one room and would have more time to study. We agreed. He also said he knew a man in the Jewish Congress who might be able to help us.

The next day we brought Eva to a school near Willy's home. She did not know French, which the children in her grade had learned for several years, so a cousin of mine offered to have her daughter tutor her until she caught up. We were grateful since we could not afford to pay a tutor and did not know enough French ourselves to help her. After a few weeks she was fine.

The Jewish Congress promised to consider our case very soon. We found a nice room with kitchen privileges and immediately moved in and began studying. Yet once again, there was fighting and commotion in our landlady's family. The mother finally confessed that her daughter was mentally ill and impossible to control and, after observing her behaviour, we determined that she was a paranoid schizophrenic. It was difficult to study under those conditions but we did our best, often closing ourselves in for 16 hours at a time and pausing only for meals.

The Jewish Congress lent us $50 for our monthly rent and $16 per week for food and other necessities. Every month one of us — usually Leon — waited hours in line to pick up our cheque of about $115. It was very little, but with Eva staying at my brother's we managed to survive on bread and coffee for breakfast and lunch and a hamburger and potatoes for supper. We couldn't afford fruit or desserts.

And so the winter passed. In April we gathered together the few hundred dollars we had carefully saved and went to take the Dominion Council Examinations. Immediately afterwards we looked for a new place to live to escape our landlady and her daughter and to be closer to Willy's so that Eva could stay with us and still attend the same school. It was difficult finding a place and we had to settle for a small room with kitchen privileges at a shoe repairman's house. I shared a single bed with Eva while Leon slept on the couch. The smell of leather from the shop below was unbearable and gave us frequent headaches, especially me. It didn't seem to bother our landlord and his wife, probably because they were conditioned to it. However, we had to stick it out until the school year was over. When I thought of the beautiful homes that Leon and I had come from, I realized how low we had fallen.

In May the results of the examinations appeared in the newspaper and our names were not among them. We had not passed. We waited anxiously for the detailed results so that we could see which subjects we had failed. We were so depressed; we had laboured so hard with the language and financial difficulties to take the exams and had given up the most essential things, to no avail. It turned out that we were required to repeat all five subjects since we had passed only two each: pathology and internal medicine for Leon, and pathology and public health for me.

After a few difficult days we consoled ourselves by saying that we had been in more difficult situations in the past and had always managed to survive. We realized that the system of examinations was very different here than in Europe and that was why we had failed, not because of lack of knowledge of medicine. We had never taken written examinations during all our years of studies in Europe, only oral ones, and we were sure that if the exams here had been oral we would have passed.

Our priorities shifted after that: we decided that the best thing for us and Eva was to concentrate on finding a job in a mental hospital. We couldn't continue to concentrate solely on passing the exams because we could not know when that would happen. We had to earn a decent salary, make a home for ourselves and our child, and stop living the miserable existence that had started in 1939 and had lasted 11 years. We had experience in psychiatry from before the war and knew a number of European doctors who, without experience or the examinations, had worked in mental hospitals for decent salaries. We sent letters of inquiry to hospitals all over the country. We also rented a relatively quiet place where Eva could have her own room.

The first reply to our letters came from a mental health director in Saint John, New Brunswick. He was very interested in our backgrounds and asked to meet us in Montreal. We wrote him back immediately, saying we eagerly awaited his call. After we met and he had looked over our credentials he assured us that he had jobs for us at a salary we would find satisfactory. He promised to send us an official confirmation shortly.

We were hopeful that we would soon find better times and continued to work hard on our studies. Eva started again in a new school. The director from Saint John had agreed that we should concentrate on our examinations for the time being and come to New Brunswick immediately after retaking them. That meant saving up the exam fees again — and living almost entirely on bread and potatoes. I remember once when I went to the bakery to buy bread with Eva. She saw a piece of chocolate cake she wanted but I had to refuse her because I knew we would have had to fast for a day or so if I bought it.

We studied feverishly as the date of the exams approached. The minute they were over Leon went to the Jewish Congress, showed them the written confirmation of our jobs, and asked them to lend us money for the train fare to Saint John, in addition to our monthly cheque. They agreed, reminding us that beginning next year we would have to start paying back the loans in monthly instalments. We again took Eva out of school, packed up, and left Montreal.

We arrived in Saint John on a Sunday morning, left our luggage in a locker at the train station, and contacted some friends of my brother. They immediately invited us to their home and offered to help us find a boarding house since we could not afford a hotel. We met the hospital administrator, Dr. Menzies, the next morning and asked for help in finding a permanent place to stay. He was a pleasant man who went out of his way to help us. He asked his secretary to phone around to find us an apartment, described the services we would be responsible for at the hospital, and introduced us to the other physicians who showed us around the hospital. Eva waited for us in our new office, reading.

The next morning Dr. Menzies helped us decide on an apartment and personally phoned the owner. He offered to lend us beds and furniture from the hospital and arranged for the hospital truck to move our things to our new apartment. We were soon settled. It was wonderful to be on our own after so many years without privacy! Our friends in Regina sent us our household goods, and as soon as we received our first paycheque, we bought living room furniture and a bed for Eva. We hired a reasonably-priced carpenter to build the rest of the things we needed. We had to be careful, though, since we had to repay our loan to the Congress, but we were quite comfortable and cozy.

By that time, Eva had started the sixth grade. She was very happy that we were in our own place, and did extremely well at school. Before Christmas vacation, her principal told us that he and her teachers thought she should move into the seventh grade when the students returned. If we agreed, they would give her additional work to do over vacation and if she did well she'd be allowed to advance. We were afraid she wouldn't have time to do all this, since we were going to spend the vacation with cousins in New York, but the principal persuaded us by saying that her teachers were forever trying to find extra work for her since she was so quick. We relented. Eva was always interested in learning new things, and immediately became engrossed in her books. A competent psychologist from Montreal who worked at our hospital gave her an I.Q. test on which she scored very high. He was also convinced that she should skip a grade or she would become bored.

We had a lovely time with our cousins in New York. A different world had opened up for us since we had come to Saint John. We finished paying for the furniture and other household goods we had bought and saved money for our vacation and buying clothes, since we had so little to wear.

We also became friendly with many people in Saint John and began to socialize again. Many of our new friends had beautiful homes, and we tried to improve our home as much as possible, as well. Eva attended Hebrew school in the afternoons and took ballet and piano lessons. She was at the head of her seventh grade class. We had a good relationship with Dr. Menzies and the rest of the staff at the hospital. It did not take long before we referred to it as "our hospital," a place where our work was appreciated.

In early spring we had some problems with our apartment; water leaked in and some of our things were damaged. The landlord promised to try to fix it, but it did not help much: rain leaked into Eva's room and it looked awful. One day Dr. Menzies told us in confidence that an apartment on the hospital grounds would soon become available and although there were other doctors who would gladly take it, he wanted to offer it to us first. The new apartment was far better than the one we had now, and its rent was cheaper, so we immediately agreed. We paid a penalty of one month's rent in our old place and prepared to move. Dr. Menzies again sent the hospital truck with moving men to help us. This move was more difficult than the previous ones because we had more breakable things that we had to pack ourselves. Once we were settled into our new home, however, we were quite content. We were closer to the hospital and could come home for lunch. The only drawback was that we had to accompany Eva to the bus stop since there were patients on the grounds and we didn't want her to walk alone.

Leon joined the Men's Zionist Organization and I the Hadassah-Wizo Organization. He served as chairman of the Negev Dinners, which pleased him very much. After the dinners, we usually had a party in our large living room for the guest of honour, the entire committee, and our close friends. We enjoyed every bit of our active lives.

The following year, when Easter vacation approached, Eva's principal again insisted that she try to advance to the ninth grade. By the end of the year, she was at the head of her class and had won all possible prizes, including a gold medal. During the summers, we sent her to Camp Kadimah in Nova Scotia. We bought a car and both tried to learn to drive, which was not easy. When Dr. Menzies retired, we were offered his apartment, which was tremendous, but we asked to have it redecorated to suit our own tastes. The new hospital administrator, Dr. Gregory, agreed because he said that we had kept our old apartment so nice that nothing had to be done to it before the new tenants could move in. We bought a piano for Eva and some new furniture and drapes. We were pleased with our new home, and had friends over often. We had a happy few years.

Eva was valedictorian at her confirmation and shared her bat mitzvah ceremony with seven other girls. She was the most fluent in Hebrew and was at the top of her class. She also did extremely well in high school. She was valedictorian of her class and came third in the province in the Junior Matriculations. At graduation she was awarded almost all the prizes. Needless to say, we were very proud of her.

While she was still in high school, however, I became very ill. I was seen by a very good internist but since all my tests came out negative, it was difficult to make a diagnosis. In less than three months, my weight had dropped to 90 pounds and I could no longer walk. My doctor suspected I had Simonds Cachexia, an incurable condition of unknown origin. He arranged for a consultation at the Lahey Clinic in Boston where I was seen by Dr. Bartells, one of the five consultants to King George. The minute he shook hands with me, Dr. Bartells diagnosed a very severe toxic form of hyperthyroidism, since my thenar muscles were gone. After many tests, he advised me to return home and try hard to gain weight — even if I had to drink a quart of cream daily — and then to return for an operation. Two weeks later, Leon and I returned to Boston where I was operated on by Dr. Catell, a surgeon who impressed me very much. I recovered quickly but could not work for almost three months. Dr. Gregory and the staff visited me frequently, and I received my full salary during this time.

Eva entered McGill University when she was 15 years old. She decided to take a combined course in Arts and Science since she was not sure which direction she would pursue. She was awarded a four-year scholarship to McGill to cover all her expenses: her stay at the Royal Victoria College, tuition, books, and pocket money. She was later awarded a General Motors scholarship of another $1100. When she came home for Christmas vacation, she told us she had been encouraged to go straight into her second year, but we advised her against it because she would be so much younger than her classmates.

We were so happy to have Eva home over the vacation. We had missed her when she left home, probably because she was so young. We began to inquire about employment in Montreal so we could all be together. Leon wrote to the Psychiatry Department at McGill but was told that they would recognize only two years of his experience in hospital psychiatry, and he would be required to do another two years in the diploma course. He was assigned to the Queen Mary Veterans' Hospital. I got a job at the Douglas Hospital, then called the Verdun Protestant Hospital. Dr. Gregory in Saint John gave Leon a year of absence with full pay — he wanted to make sure he would return — and after much discussion, a year of leave for me, too, but without pay.

And so we moved to Montreal. My first day at work was a hard one. One of the chief doctors, who showed me around the hospital, never stopped running and I had a difficult time keeping up with him. I was told that my duties included looking after the infirmary, the staff clinic, and a geriatric floor. I objected to this because I had worked as a psychiatrist for a number of years and was out of touch with these areas of medicine, but I was told that someone had to do it and that someone was me. There was a world of difference between the humane approach in Saint John and this hospital in Montreal. I felt really depressed.

17

ALTHOUGH WE WERE FREE to return to Saint John at any time, we decided to give our new lives in Montreal a try. We wanted to be closer to Eva. We stayed temporarily in an apartment house on Dorchester Street, which rented small flats on a weekly basis, but after we realized what a poor neighbourhood it was in, we looked for another place.

The duty roster at work came out and I saw that I had been put on a first call schedule along with the residents; I had to stay in the hospital from 5:00 p.m. until 8:30 a.m., looking after all emergencies and admissions, and then work through the next day. I could not complain to the Director, whom I had met the previous day and considered one of the most unreasonable men I had ever met. Instead, I spoke to his secretary, who noted my surprise that as a staff member I was placed on first call. She agreed that this was unfair, and promised to point out my complaint to the Director. The next thing I knew I was told by the secretary that the schedule would be changed for the next month. I am sure that if I had talked to him myself he would have found some excuse not to change it, but he was probably ashamed of his unfairness in front of the secretary.

I stuck it out for the month of nights spent sleeping at the hospital.

We found a comfortable furnished apartment on Atwater Street. We took it on a monthly basis so we could look for a permanent place for all of us when Eva returned from her summer job as a counsellor at Camp Kadimah. For the next month we continued looking for a proper apartment and finally decided on one near Leon's hospital and not too far from McGill, but quite a distance from my own hospital. It was poorly furnished but we settled there for the year. It was hard for me to keep house because I spent a lot of time travelling to and from the hospital and was tired when I got home.

At the hospital, I ran the infirmary and the other services assigned to me. I also had to arrange for operations and notify anaesthesiologists, which often took a lot of time. I had to inform relatives, get consents for operations and autopsies, deal with the public curator, and do many other jobs. Conditions at the hospital were extremely difficult at the time. For years, only the executives and two senior psychiatrists had their own offices; the rest of the staff doctors and the residents had to do their work on noisy wards, nursing stations, or in the very busy medical records office. When I complained once, I was told that there was a small place under a staircase that I could use, so I tried it. It was a tiny dark hole under busy stairs with people constantly clattering up and down, and it was impossible to concentrate.

I arranged to take my vacation during the month of July, after which we knew that we would have to return to Saint John to fulfil our obligations. I decided to ask for a year's absence — explaining to the hospital in Montreal that I had taken a year off in Saint John and had to return — so that I would have enough time to liquidate our apartment in Saint John. We bought a home in Montreal that was unfinished inside. For weeks we spent every free moment working with the builders until the lower flat was finished and we could rent it. When the upper flat was ready, about two months later, we rented it as well. At the end of the year I was granted the leave of absence, but was given only two weeks of vacation instead of a month. We were disappointed at having to shorten our vacation after such a difficult year, and at having to cancel hotel reservations and lose money.

On the first of August, we returned to Saint John and resumed our apartment and duties. Though we were very happy there, we had already decided to return to Montreal — and to Eva and our new home. We left our hospital on very good terms and with strong letters of recommendation. While we were in Saint John, a new superintendent had been appointed at Douglas Hospital. When I returned to work, I expected to run the geriatric ward and staff clinic, as had been previously confirmed, but was told that I was to take on the infirmary as well. I went to see the new administrator, and he reluctantly agreed to find someone else to take over the infirmary.

The next year at the hospital went more smoothly; I was working with young chronic patients, which suited me much better. Yet life at home was not quite as settled. We moved into our new house, bought some mattresses to sleep on and borrowed a bridge table and chairs from my sister to eat on, but the house was mostly empty. We spent every free moment looking for furnishings and taking care of the garden and lawn. We were extremely busy but also happy, looking forward to a comfortable life in our new home. We began socializing and dreamed of saving money for travel. However, things did not turn out according to our wishes.

Leon finished the Diploma Course and tried to work in private practice. It was hard to get referrals from established psychiatrists, and since there was no Medicare it was difficult to expect payment from many of the indigent patients. The Douglas Hospital offered him a job looking after the infirmary and a geriatric ward. He hesitated; after all, he was a certified psychiatrist by then and wanted to be doing psychiatry. Yet since he knew medicine quite well, he would just need to brush up on the latest treatments and drugs and would have no difficulty with the infirmary. He accepted, making it clear to the hospital administration that he would only be filling in until a position in psychiatry became available.

When one did open up, however, it was given to someone else, upsetting Leon very much. He was also annoyed at being treated like a child at the hospital by one of the seniors, who monitored everyone's comings and goings. Leon was unhappy with the conditions at the hospital, but tried to play by their rules. Therefore, when he was told by the administration that there would not be a position for him for the following year, he was shocked. He had worked under the Germans and Soviets, in hospitals in Poland and Austria, and could not understand how they could do this to him now. He wondered day and night about what he had said or done wrong, but could think of nothing. He approached another administrator for a recommendation so that he could try to find work elsewhere, and was given a glowing one. Even the administrator who checked everyone's comings and goings told me it was a surprise to him that Leon was not offered a position there.

I decided to see the administrator after he had refused to see Leon. He told me that Leon did not fit into the organization, but when I pressed for details, he refused to say more. Leon was bewildered and depressed. He could not sleep or eat and he looked sick. When he started looking around Montreal for another job, we realized that the administrator had closed every door to him. The only reason we could think of was his anti-Semitism, which we had heard of in another case as well. Other physicians on staff who did not possess a fraction of Leon's intelligence and sense of duty had worked for years at the Douglas Hospital, doing very superficial jobs and never really fulfilling their duties.

Leon was so bitterly disappointed that he decided to ask for a job in Saint John, where he was accepted with open arms. When the year at the Douglas was finished he left to work there. He wanted me to liquidate everything in Montreal and come with him, but it was not so easy. Eva had been accepted into medical school at McGill by this time and was living at home. We had put so much hard work into building our home that it was difficult to leave it. I decided to remain in Montreal for a year to see if a job would turn up for Leon and he could return.

Leon visited us for a few days whenever he could, and Eva and I did the same. Yet it wasn't enough. We had never been separated before and I missed him very much. On one of his visits I noticed that he did not look well and had become very thin. He confessed that he had noticed an enlarged lymph node about the size of a pea on the right side of his jaw. I insisted he go for a biopsy. It proved positive, and a diagnosis of lymphosarcoma was made. He was referred to Dr. Lowenstein, an excellent haematologist and a marvellous human being.

As for me, the world was over. Leon and I had been together since I had started medical school at the age of 19. We grew up together — came to like or dislike the same things — and I could not imagine life without him. The months he spent in Saint John were very difficult for me, despite frequent phone calls and visits.

Dr. Lowenstein called me to the hospital without Leon's knowledge. He asked if I wanted Leon to know the truth about his condition. I said no, definitely not, because although the saying goes, "where there is life there is hope," I believed also that "where there is hope there is life." The doctor thought Leon might live two or three years, no more. We agreed that he would tell him that he had made a diagnosis of Giant Follicular Lymphoma, a borderline condition that is treated the same way as a malignancy to prevent it from turning malignant. Most people could live about 20 years before it would turn malignant.

I was shocked and depressed but determined to live our lives as before. I explained to Leon that the most important thing was that he stay in Montreal for treatment and get well. I also told him that he should only accept patients who could come to his office at home. He had become interested in working up cases for restitution purposes and had quite a number of referrals.

I secretly contacted Dr. Gregory, the administrator at the hospital in Saint John, who immediately wrote me back saying that he would arrange sick leave for my husband so that he would receive his regular salary for the next six months. If he needed more time, he could receive his pension after that time. He later wrote to Leon, telling him the same thing, in a letter that sounded like one from a father to his son.

Leon was more relaxed after Dr. Gregory's reassurances, and he started radiation therapy. After the third treatment, he became sicker than anyone I had ever seen in all the years I worked in hospitals. He could not sit up in bed; his mouth and throat were chapped, as well as the skin on his legs, arms, and buttocks. Sheets of skin came off and his sore muscles underneath were exposed. Dr. Lowenstein examined him and expressed fear that he would contract pneumonia, but warned that the danger of getting it in the hospital would be even greater.

I was given a month's vacation and stayed at home with Leon. At first I used an eyedropper to feed him fluids. To prevent him from getting bedsores, I changed his position frequently, keeping him on a padded rubber ring. I was constantly at his side, giving him hope. After about two weeks, he was able to eat mashed food and sit propped up with pillows. A week later he was able to take a few steps to reach the bathroom. He urged me to return to work, assuring that he could manage without me.

I decided to try. I left him food in the refrigerator and some drinks and cookies near the bed. I phoned him from work whenever I had a chance. Eva tried to come home whenever she could to give him lunch and to be with him. We had a good tenant who was a registered nurse and she also checked in on Leon periodically. Gradually he was able to walk more and care for himself. Dr. Lowenstein urged him to begin the radiation treatments again, but Leon was understandably reluctant to do so. He spoke to the radiologist who admitted that Leon had mistakenly been given an overdose of radiation the first time, which was what caused him to be so ill. He assured him that it would not happen again. With great hesitation Leon returned to his treatments. This time they went more smoothly.

18

DURING THE WINTER Leon went out only for his radiation treatments. He gradually regained some weight. He also started to become restless and began to see restitution cases again. It was frequently noted how well he worked up his patients, not only as a psychiatrist but also as a lawyer, defending their rights to compensation. His cases were almost never refused.

When spring came, he was well into remission and I talked with Eva about taking a trip to Israel, something Leon had long dreamed of. We decided to go to Europe as well, and I arranged for time off from the hospital. We left in the summer of 1961. Leon was feeling better and we all looked forward to a much desired long vacation. We went first to London. As

I was getting off a bus one day it suddenly started to move and I was dragged on the ground for some distance. My left foot was badly injured, and I was taken to a hospital, where it was determined that I had torn a tendon. My foot was blue and swollen. We stayed in London longer than we had planned while I recovered, then left for Paris. There, we rented a car and saw a lot of the city and its outskirts before continuing on to Switzerland, which was clean in contrast to Paris and where the people were much more polite and friendly. From there we went to Rome, Milan, and Venice. Finally, Eva had to return to Montreal to start her summer job and Leon and I flew to Israel.

Our reception in Israel remains vivid in my memory. We arrived at Lod Airport on a very hot afternoon. The plane was filled to capacity and the crowd at the airport was huge. Suddenly we heard "Dr. Deutsch" called over the loudspeaker. A man approached us, cleared us through passport control, asked for our luggage, and told us to follow him outside. He introduced himself as a representative of the Minister of Health, who had been a close school friend of Leon. The Minister of Health had heard from other friends of ours that we were arriving, and had sent his official to greet us. More than 60 other friends and relatives also met us at the airport, and each one invited us to stay at their homes. We finally decided to stay with Leon's uncle, so as not to insult him. We promised to see the others during our visit.

After seeing friends in the Tel Aviv area, we toured the rest of the beautiful country, always returning on weekends to my best friend from college, Fryda Frydman, who lived in a nice villa in Ramat Gan. She and her husband took us to beautiful beaches, concerts, operas, plays and movies. Leon felt well except for one day when he developed a high fever. I immediately phoned a haematologist whom Dr. Lowenstein had recommended before we left. The next day his temperature was normal and he felt his usual self. Though we greatly enjoyed our stay in Israel, at the back of my mind was always the worry that Leon would get sick. I also frequently found myself wondering if we had made a mistake by immigrating to Canada instead of Israel. Leon had been an ardent Zionist since his youth — and a leader of the youth movement Hanoar Ha'Ivri — and all his school friends had looked up to him. Those very same friends now occupied high positions in the Israeli government. We would certainly have had an easier time establishing ourselves in Israel, since we knew so many people who respected us. Leon could have reached a high position in his profession, and I could have worked in a hospital that I liked. Yet I had longed for my relatives in Canada and could not have foreseen the hardships we encountered there. We had tried to leave for Israel once, before we got our positions in Saint John, but didn't have money for the fare. Then later, even Leon thought we had wandered enough.

When we left Israel, we toured Europe some more and came home. The next year was full of ups and downs with regard to Leon's health. He tried to do some private practice, and continued seeing the restitution cases, but he developed severe pain in his legs and his chemotherapy was increased. The side effects were not as bad as they had been with the first radiation treatment, however, and he managed to continue working. By spring he was in remission again and seemed to be doing well by the summer and fall.

We received an invitation from close cousins in Chile, so I took another accumulated vacation and we left for Mexico City. From there we went to South America, to Peru, to visit my cousin in Argentina, and to Uruguay, where my sister-in-law had family. We saw Brazil and Barbados and Bermuda. From there we flew home. I was thankful that Leon and I were able to travel so much and to meet so many of our relatives while he was still well enough to do so.

19

EVA GRADUATED from McGill medical school in 1963. With the quotas then she was the only Jewish female in her class. Leon was working and feeling all right and life returned to normal — we were invited out often and enjoyed socializing in our home. When winter came and I had accumulated more vacation, we decided to take a cruise. We took the Empress of Canada to Grenada, Curaçao, and St. Thomas. On the way back Leon became extremely ill. He could not even sit up, but when I brought the ship's doctor he just said "Let's hope he can stick it out." When we arrived back in New York, Leon was taken off the ship in a wheelchair. He was so weak that we had to spend the night at the airport until Leon's cousin, Alfred, could come and help us to the train station to return to Canada. Leon lay in the train groaning, while I counted the hours and minutes until we returned to Montreal. Eva was waiting for us at the station and together we managed to get him into bed at home.

I nursed him and he continued his chemotherapy until he was well enough for me to return to work. He gradually managed to work a bit, but at one point had to spend two weeks in the hospital.

The following year, 1965, Eva announced her engagement. We knew how badly Leon wanted to see her married, so we decided to have the wedding on 19 September, before the High Holy Days. Leon did much of the searching for the synagogue and other arrangements for the wedding, though he did not feel well. The wedding weekend was a lovely affair, full of out-of-town guests and friends, and well worth all the effort.

Eva and her new husband Frederick left for their

honeymoon. The next day our upstairs tenant moved out and we decided it would be better for us to live there because the lower flat was too large for us, especially when Leon was in the hospital and I was alone. In the middle of everything, Leon became very ill with severe headaches and pain in his gums. It was difficult for him to eat or drink and he could hardly sit up in bed. I spent a week running from his bedside to the flat upstairs to supervise the painters, plasterers, and other workers as they prepared the flat for us and worked on ours, as well, for the next tenants. It took a good six weeks to get completely moved in, since I was working every day and had only evenings and some weekends free.

Leon improved and life resumed. We tried to take it easy, but I worked regularly and Leon took on a tremendous number of restitution cases along with his private practice. Eva and her husband returned from their honeymoon and moved into their new apartment. She was doing her post-graduate degree in genetics and was quite busy. They would come over for supper once or twice a week, and we would occasionally go out together. And so the winter set in. Every few weeks Leon would feel ill again, each time with something else: his heart, a ruptured spleen, etc. He used to say, "in the last year I am more sick than well."

When spring approached I was afraid that Leon would want to have a large seder at our home, as he always did. We would invite about 20 people over and they were always impressed by his beautiful singing, interpretations, and explanations. We did extensive cleaning before the holiday, and always got new clothes for the seder, but it was always worth the extra effort. I didn't even want to talk about Passover that year; I was so afraid that Leon would get sick at the last moment and we would have to call off the seder. Our friends would understand, but this was a special evening: a national holiday when we became a nation and every Jew feels like being together with his close friends and relatives. It is unthinkable to be alone during that evening.

About two weeks before the seder, Leon told me that since he was not feeling so well he thought we should just have Eva, her husband, and his family for the seder. He began to conduct the evening but quickly developed severe abdominal pain and had to lie down. I served our guests supper and from time to time looked in on him. I was glad when the evening was over.

The cycle continued. Leon would feel better, then have a relapse. During a good period we decided to attend the World Congress of Psychiatry in Madrid, Spain, stopping on the way to meet Leon's cousin Kuba and his wife Trudy in Paris. We had a lovely time in both places. I was so happy that Leon could enjoy everything, but I did notice that he was easily irritated, which was unlike him. On the way back we made a stop in beautiful Algiers, and from there the trip home deteriorated. We had to wait a very long time for a plane home from Paris, and we were both exhausted. I went to work the next day and when I called Leon at lunchtime he told me he had developed severe diarrhoea. He lost weight rapidly and we could not control the diarrhoea for about ten days, but after that he again recovered.

Shortly afterwards he developed a low-grade fever and was admitted to the hospital by the haematologist. On the weekend no tests were done and he was allowed to go home. On Sunday we went with Eva and her husband to see the Expo '67 site, which was then being constructed. Afterwards he told me how glad he was to have seen it. That night he went back to the hospital for the last time.

The next morning he developed a high fever. The resident and the nurses tried to cool him down by opening all the windows and making a draft with towels, while Leon lay naked on the bed. In the evening the haematologist's assistant told him he had pneumonia. Leon replied, "This is the end. I do not have the resistance to fight pneumonia." I was annoyed that he had been told the truth; I saw no need for it.

From then on he talked constantly about his death. He told me what to do after he died and repeatedly said that if Eva gave birth to a girl, he would like her to be named after his mother. He wanted me to go to Israel the following February, as we had planned, to put up a monument for his family. It was unbearable to listen to him talk constantly. I called his cousin Kuba to his bedside, which helped somewhat, but he had to return to New York the same evening. The next day Leon again talked constantly and realized himself that he could not stop. I spent the night in the hospital and when I entered his room the next morning he told me that he was surprised he had survived the night.

Around nine o'clock that evening Eva came and made me go home because I was so tired. The minute I got home the phone rang and it was Leon. He said he had something important to say. I told him that I would like to take my coat off and lie down and that he should call back in a few minutes. He never did. I called the hospital but the switchboard refused to phone his room since it was after hours.

I rushed to the hospital early the next morning. Leon was exhausted and unable to speak. Around noon he went into a seizure and was taken to intensive care. He was unconscious for the rest of that day and all night. In the morning, when I went to his room, he opened his eyes. When the haematologist came he was even able to lift his hand, touch his nose, and do all the things the doctor asked. It was miraculous. At one point he motioned for me to bring him a piece of paper and a pen, which I did. The first word he wrote out, larynx, was legible, but the rest was not. I kept that piece of paper to this day.

In the middle of the night Leon's blood pressure fell drastically. Early the next morning, after the physicians made their rounds, I stopped by the room and saw a nurse disconnecting the respirator. My husband had died. My pain was so unbearable that all I wanted to do was be with Eva. I ran out to find her.

Our relatives from New York came to the funeral, and then Eva and I sat shiva for a week. People came and went all day, expressing their condolences and praying with us at established times. A colleague of mine who had never attended a shiva was astonished to see how many people were at my house.

When the week of shiva was over, Eva returned to her apartment and my loneliness began. I sat alone in our large place, often talking loudly to my husband, afraid the neighbours would overhear. I was desperate and ached all over from loneliness. I only felt comfort when I was with my daughter, but she was busy with her work and her husband and home so I didn't see her too often. It took a while until I was able to resume my daily business, and settle all matters of insurance and the like.

As I had promised Leon, I travelled to Israel to have the tree-planting ceremony for his family. It took place in a forest midway between Tel Aviv and Jerusalem, in Yaar Hertzl, Ben Shemen. The ceremony was beautifully conducted by Keren Kayemet, and many people came to speak about their friendships with Leon. When I unveiled the monument even I was impressed with its beauty. Each time I go to Israel I see the forest and admire how fast it has grown.

I returned to Canada and to work, though I still didn't feel like facing people and I usually ate lunch alone rather than join others in the cafeteria. A few months later, my first grandchild was born and she eased my loneliness somewhat. I frequently stayed with her on weekends when Eva and Frederick were away at medical conferences.

When summer came, I began to look for a headstone for Leon's grave. Eva and I decided on black African marble and a large stone for both of our graves. We also decided to engrave the names of Leon's and my parents and siblings on the bottom of the headstone so that at least their names would be remembered. Many of our friends and relatives came to the unveiling that fall on a day that was very difficult for both me and Eva.

It still wasn't enough. I wanted to do more for Leon, for a man with such intelligence and ability that some record should be left behind, if only for his grandchildren. I had been thinking about the 700 histories of Holocaust survivors that he had worked up for restitution purposes but had been unable to compile into a book, as he had planned, because of his health. A colleague of ours, a fine psychiatrist and friend, agreed to coedit the book with me, and together with Eva we selected 50 histories to publish. We added chapters on various aspects of the Holocaust and its psychiatric consequences, which were written by experts in the field. We continued to work on this for several years.

Passover approached. Eva and Frederick decided to spend the holiday in Jamaica, which suited me fine; I was not ready to sit at a seder like I had done so many times before with Leon, surrounded by our family and friends. The week of Passover I came home from work each evening and ate dinner alone in the kitchen. I spoke only to my friends when they called.

20

THE YEARS PASSED. I worked long hours in the hospital where I was chief of a large service that consisted of more than 400 patients. In addition to my clinical work I undertook several research projects in Psychopharmacology with two well-known researchers, Dr. Heinz Lehmann and Dr. Thomas Ban. I enjoyed this so much that when I was offered a full-time position in research, I retired from my staff position at the hospital and accepted. I eventually became coordinator of the Research Department at the Douglas, where I worked for nearly six years, until the Department was dissolved and I returned to my previous office. However, I continued to work with Dr. Lehmann as a Research Associate in the Department of Psychopharmacology at McGill University for another ten years.

We worked on several projects, including five- and ten-year follow-up studies on depressed patients for the World Health Organization (WHO) in Geneva.

In June, 1977, my grandson Mark was born, and I spent any free time I had after work helping Eva with the children. Eva was chief of the Genetics Department at the Montreal Neurological Institute and she and Frederick had to travel to conferences frequently while I stayed with the children. I acquired an office at the Montreal General Hospital, since many of the depressed patients came from there, and began another project for the WHO, detecting depressed patients in a general practitioner's office.

In 1979, I decided to sell my house and move into an apartment. This proved quite difficult, and after I finally moved I became quite ill. It took about four months until I felt like myself again and could continue to work.

My grandchildren were a great source of pleasure and comfort for me. My oldest granddaughter, Lisa, had her Bat Mitzvah, which she did very well, and later had her high school graduation. My younger granddaughter, Annie, took part in several plays, including *Oliver* and *Oklahoma*, and I enjoyed watching her act.

Once I felt well enough, I travelled again to Israel. From there I went to Egypt for a week, and then to the International Congress of Psychiatry in Vienna. Although I had planned to meet Eva and Frederick and the children in Vienna, I didn't know which hotel they were staying in, so after checking into my hotel, I went for a walk in the park near the Congress. Coincidentally, my grandson Mark was waiting for his mother in the same park when he saw me approach, and he immediately jumped up and ran over to begin kissing me and shouting in joy. I had not seen him in three weeks, and he kept repeating, "It's been so long since I've seen you! It's been so long since I've seen you!"

21

A FEW YEARS LATER I arranged another trip to Israel, this one with Eva, Frederick, and the children, so that they could attend the dedication of the chair in Psychopharmacology at the Hebrew University, which had been named for Leon and myself. It had long been a dream of mine. The entire family left for Israel on 13 May 1985. On 23 May the Dean of the Faculty of Medicine presented me with my citation, followed by a short speech by me and a longer one by Eva. Friends and relatives came from all over, despite a *hamsin* (a hot dry wind) that day. I was overjoyed that my wish had finally been fulfilled.

After we returned from Israel, Annie graduated at

the top of her class from elementary school. It was a beautiful ceremony. Shortly after that she had her Bat Mitzvah, which she performed excellently. She as well as Mark, who was eight years old at the time, gave nice speeches at a celebration dinner that evening.

The years 1989 and 1990 were also full of accomplishments by my grandchildren. First, Lisa graduated in Anthropology with distinction from McGill University. Annie graduated as valedictorian and Head Girl from her high school. She received the Governor General's Medal. On 16 June 1990, Mark had his Bar Mitzvah. He delivered his haftorah exceptionally well. Although a marvellous simcha followed, I could not enjoy it entirely because I had lost my brother Willy just a few weeks before. Yet the event gave me great pleasure, as do all my grandchildren's accomplishments.

Lisa received an M.Phil. degree in Social Anthropology from the University of Cambridge in 1992. Her dissertation was on Ethiopian Jews, and she has since continued her research in medical anthropology of Ethiopian Jews in Israel. Lisa is now in her second year of medicine at McGill University. Anne spent a semester studying abroad at The Hebrew University of Jerusalem, and had a wonderful time. She is graduating this year from McGill University in Honours Biology, and is on the Dean's Honour List. Anne was awarded the Philip F. Vineberg Travelling Fellowship in order to pursue graduate studies at the Wellcome Unit for the History of Medicine in Cambridge, before starting the following year at McGill Medical School. Mark is graduating this year from high school, and is doing extremely well. His Headmaster's comments on his December report card are worth quoting: "Mark has had an outstanding term in all respects and is to be congratulated. His consistently high marks for effort are particularly impressive. His perfect score in physics for both term work and the examination is an accomplishment I have not seen previously." He was also elected to the Cum Laude Society, based on his academic excellence, good character, honour, and integrity in all aspects of school life.

To this day, my grandchildren are the most important part of my life.

My parents, Pesach and Taube (Liebling) Kimmel, circa 1931.

My in-laws, Moses and Fanny (Grunfeld) Deutsch, with two of their three children, Leon and his younger sister Ida, a few years before the war.

My late husband Leon (bottom, centre), leader of the Zionist Youth Movement (Hanoar Haivri), Przemyśl, 1930. His good friend David Gazith is at top left.

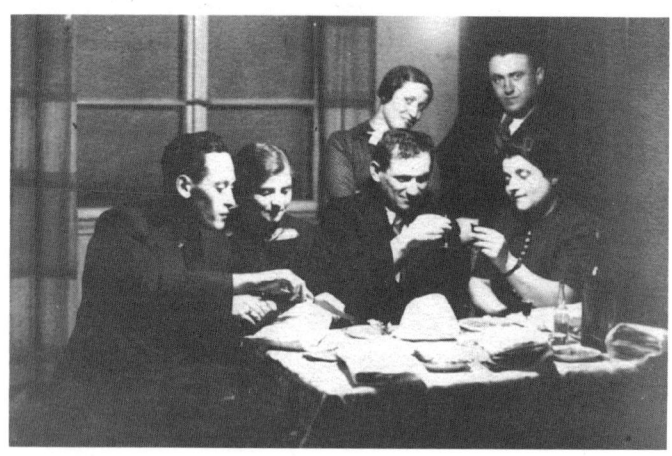

A Passover seder in Prague that I prepared for Leon and some of my other friends from medical school.

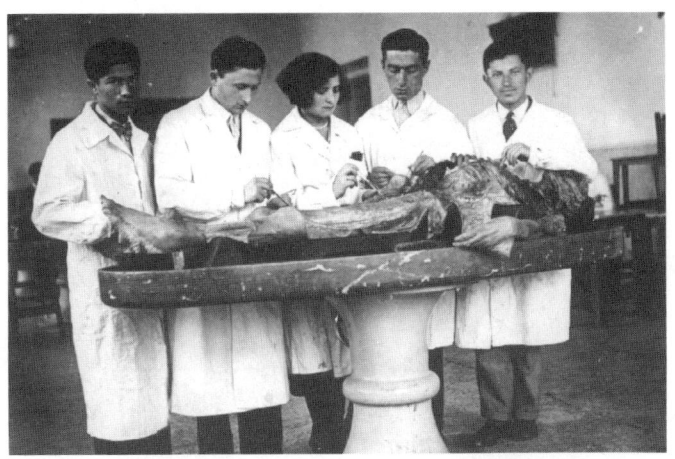

Dissecting a cadaver with colleagues at the University in Prague, Czechoslovakia circa 1933.

This photo of me standing in front of my boarding house on Karlove Namesti was taken by Leon during our university days in Prague.

Our engagement photo, Prague, February 1938.

Our wedding picture, Lwów, September 1938.

Leon's home in Przemyśl where our daughter Eva was born on 19 October 1939, six weeks after the outbreak of the war.

My sister-in-law Ida at the piano shortly before the war. She perished in Auschwitz of typhoid fever.

Leon with his older brother Romek, who perished in the gas chambers in Auschwitz.

My oldest sister Lottie's children, Markus and Eva, 1931. They both perished with their mother in the Borszczów ghetto at the ages of 18 and 13.

Members of my family before the war. Left to right: Myself, Lottie, my mother, Regina and her husband Isidore. I am the only survivor.

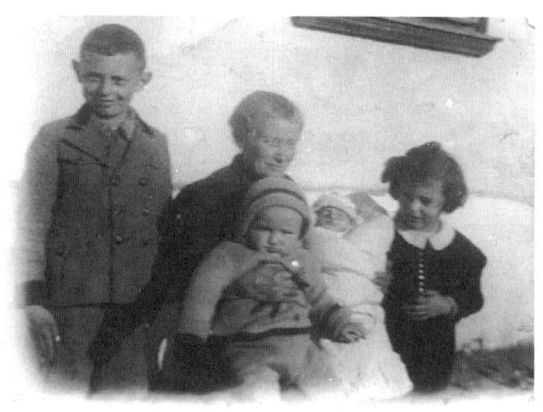

My mother, Taube Kimmel, surrounded by her grandchildren: (from left) Markus, Philip, Julek, and Eva, 1935.

My younger brother Levi standing by my side in Mielnica shortly before the war. He perished in the Borszczów ghetto at the age of 28, in 1943.

My daughter, Eva, wearing a dress that I sewed from a white parachute which I found after the end of the fighting, Katowice, 1946.

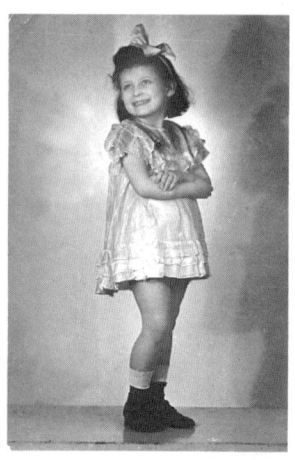

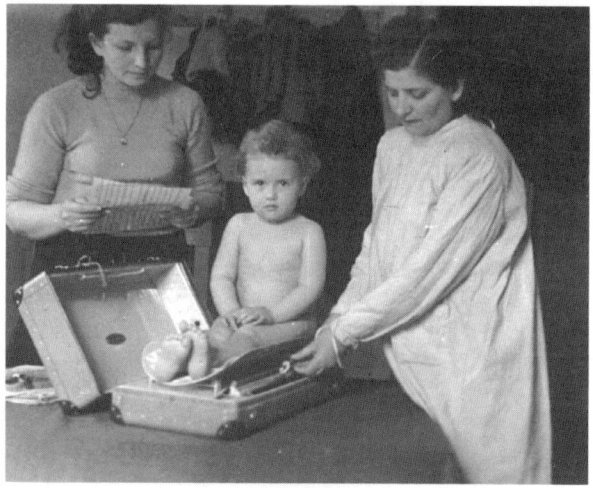

This photograph of me (right) working as a camp doctor in Camp Riedenburg, Salzburg, Austria, 1947, was taken by the Joint Distribution Committee, and appeared in a number of American newspapers.

Eva and I (right, front), soon after our arrival in Canada, with my brother Willy, his wife Lily, and their son Earl (back row) and daughter Miriam (left, front), 1948.

My sister, Rachel, her husband, Baruch, and their son, Philip, who survived the war with us in the bunker. This photo was taken in Montreal where they settled after the war.

THE EVENING TIMES-GLOBE, SAINT JOHN, N. B., FRIDAY,

Honored At Negev Dinner

Left to right: Mrs. Leon Deutsch, Dr. Deutsch, A. Calp, Shoshana Shushan, Gdalia Zakiff, Joshua Lieberman.

Prominent in many spheres of community life, and for 15 years local chairman of the Jewish National Fund, Mr. Calp was guest of honor last night at the annual Negev dinner Saint John's Jewish community. Here, he shows to Israeli opera star Shoshana Shushan citation presented to him. Mr. Zakiff was the evening's principal speaker.

Leon, as Chairman of the Negev Dinner in Saint John, New Brunswick, May 1955.

*My daughter's wedding photo, September 1965.
From left to right: Leon, myself, Eva, her
husband Frederick Andermann, Fred's aunt
Julia Hubner, and Fred's mother Anny.*

At my husband's memorial service, where I dedicated a Jewish National Fund forest in his memory, Yaar Hertzl Ben Shemen, Israel, 1967.

My first grandchild, Lisa, born 12 May 1967, and named after my late husband Leon who died of cancer during my daughter's pregnancy.

At a meeting at the Douglas Hospital, where I worked as a psychiatrist and researcher for over 20 years, with Dr. Lehmann (wearing dark glasses).

Riding on an elephant during my trip to India, Jaipur, 1974.

The establishment of the Chair in Psychopharmacology at the Hebrew University of Jerusalem, May 1985. I am shaking hands with the Dean of the Faculty of Medicine, Professor Rami Rahamimoff, during the inaugural ceremony. My daughter Eva is at right.

My daughter Eva (centre) with (from left to right) her son Mark, elder daughter Lisa, husband Fred, and younger daughter Anne, 1990.

My grandchildren and I (from left to right) Anne, Lisa and Mark. This photograph was taken on the occasion of Mark's Bar Mitzvah, June 1990.

My grandchildren, Anne, Mark and Lisa, 1992.

ABOUT THE AUTHOR

Dr. Mina Deutsch was born on 24 December 1911, in Jezierżany, a small town in Galicia, which at that time was a province of the Austro-Hungarian empire. She was one of six children in a middle-class Jewish family. In 1931, she entered medical school at the German University in Prague, where she met her future husband, Leon, also a medical student.

Because of the increasing Nazi influence in Czechoslovakia, Mina and Leon returned to Poland after completing their degrees, and were married in 1938. They began to work in a psychiatric hospital near Warsaw, but soon after had to flee eastward to Przemyśl, Leon's hometown, where their daughter Eva was born six weeks after the outbreak of World War II.

During the Nazi regime, Mina and Leon were enlisted to fight a typhus epidemic in Eastern Poland. Eventually they were forced into hiding, and had many narrow escapes from death. Most members of both their families did not survive the war.

After the war, Mina and her family spent eighteen months in a DP camp in Salzburg, Austria, before emigrating to Canada in 1948. She lived in Regina, Saskatchewan, and Saint John, New Brunswick before moving to Montreal where she worked as a staff psychiatrist and researcher at the Douglas Hospital for over 20 years.

Mina continued working on research projects in the Department of Psychopharmacology at McGill University into her mid-seventies, and was an author of over twenty scientific publications. She was always a strong supporter of Israel, and is on the International Board of Governors of The Hebrew University of Jerusalem. Leon died of cancer in 1966, and Mina is now retired and living in Montreal near her daughter and grandchildren.